W9-ASI-945

Shadow Lives

SHADOW LIVES

The Forgotten Women of the War on Terror

Victoria Brittain

Foreword by John Berger
Afterword by Marina Warner

PlutoPress
www.plutobooks.com

First published 2013 by Pluto Press
345 Archway Road, London N6 5AA

www.plutobooks.com

Distributed in the United States of America exclusively by
Palgrave Macmillan, a division of St. Martin's Press LLC,
175 Fifth Avenue, New York, NY 10010

Copyright © Victoria Brittain 2013; Foreword © John Berger 2013;
Afterword © Marina Warner 2013

The right of Victoria Brittain to be identified as the author of this work has been
asserted by her in accordance with the Copyright, Designs and Patents Act 1988.

British Library Cataloguing in Publication Data
A catalogue record for this book is available from the British Library

ISBN   978 0 7453 3327 4   Hardback
ISBN   978 0 7453 3326 7   Paperback
ISBN   978 1 8496 4851 6   PDF eBook
ISBN   978 1 8496 4853 0   Kindle eBook
ISBN   978 1 8496 4852 3   EPUB eBook

Library of Congress Cataloging in Publication Data applied for

This book is printed on paper suitable for recycling and made from fully managed
and sustained forest sources. Logging, pulping and manufacturing processes are
expected to conform to the environmental standards of the country of origin.

10   9   8   7   6   5   4   3   2

Typeset from disk by Stanford DTP Services, Northampton, England
Simultaneously printed digitally by CPI Antony Rowe, Chippenham, UK and
Edwards Bros in the United States of America

For the young Palestinian women, Noor, Mariam, Laila, Sarraa, Romaitha and Aisha, for your grace and bravery

Contents

Acknowledgements   viii
Foreword by John Berger   ix

Introduction   1

1   Sabah: From Palestine to Guantanamo   24

2   Zinnira: From Medina to Guantanamo   41

3   Dina and Josephine: From Palestine and Africa
    to House Arrest in London   50

4   Hamda: From Jordan to Belmarsh Prison   68

5   Ragaa: From Egypt to Long Lartin Prison   81

6   The South London Families   98

7   Daughters and Sisters   113

8   Families Surviving the War on Terror   139

Afterword by Marina Warner   165
Notes   169
Select Bibliography   173
Index   175

Acknowledgements

My thanks go firstly to all the women in this book, several of whom have been my valued friends over several years, while others decided to tell me their stories when they heard about the book, and often became friends. Their trust that I could both tell their truth and safeguard their privacy gave me the confidence to write.

Nancy Murray and Liz Fekete patiently gave generous time to read early drafts, made many improvements to the content and structure, and were endlessly clear sighted over difficult choices about what should not go in. Michael Ratner's enthusiasm and encyclopaedic knowledge added an American dimension that I would not have dreamed of trying without his warm encouragement.

Many people have helped me in different ways with their time, their expertise and their support over the years as this project gestated, and I am very grateful to them all. Among them are Maliheh Afnan, Harmit Athwal, Moazzam Begg, Zaynab Begg, John Berger, Geoffrey Bindman, Jenny Bourne, Adrienne Burrows, Louise Christian, Augusta Conchiglia, Ibrahim Darwish, Joshua Dratel, Sally Eberhart, Catherine Freeman, the Kazmi family, Helena Kennedy, Sharhabeel Lone, Pauline Lord, Arzu Merali, Linda Moreno, Majed Nehmé, Irene Nembhard, Angela Neustatter, Helen Oldfield, Melanie Patrick, Gareth Peirce, Asim Qureshi, Noor Ravalia, Saiyeda Ravalia, Patsy Robertson, Sonali and Sharmin Sadequee, Donald Sassoon, David Shulman, A. Sivanandan, Jeanne Theoharis, Charles Tripp, Marina Warner, Frances Webber, Tom Wilner, Roger Van Zwanenberg and all my colleagues at the Institute of Race Relations.

There are some people in the book who I did not name, either to protect them or others. You know how much you have helped me – thank you.

And special thanks to Cas, Zuzana, Thea, Paul and Jessie.

Foreword

John Berger

Here is a book that contains its subject as the walls of a living room contain the lives of those who live in it. The walls don't argue, they bear witness and they listen. The lives involved here are those of Islamic women and men who have been rounded up and kept under surveillance by state officials and state bodies engaged in the so-called war on terror. The room is mostly in London and Guantanamo (Cuba) is in the basement.

What makes the book unforgettable and terrible is its demonstration of the extent of the human cruelty meted out by the (human) stupidity of those wielding power. Neither such cruelty nor such stupidity exist in the natural world without humankind.

Within the four walls of this living room we are forced to acknowledge that, although traditionally the Devil may be cunning, the humanly diabolic is, more often than not, crass, arm-twisting, overbearing and pointless.

Introduction

'You have to be very careful how you speak to these men – they've survived traumas they don't even tell about ... I see my husband struggling. The kids are struggling. It's hard ... it's hard, every single day.'[1]

Shadow Lives provides a glimpse into the world of a number of women who have had their lives shattered by the myths and fables generated by the war on terror and the new geopolitics. These myths and fables shape everyday perceptions about refugees and those displaced from countries such as Afghanistan, Egypt, Jordan and Palestine, and blind us to the injustice meted out under our anti-terrorist laws, in the name of our national security. Much of the background to their story begins in Afghanistan, a country of myth and fable for centuries, and a magnet for invaders from Alexander the Great in 330 BC, to the British imperial ambitions in the mid-nineteenth century, before the Soviet Union and the Americans took the same route.

Afghanistan has been devastated for its own Afghan people many times over, but worst of all in the most ideological and technological of wars that started as the opening salvo of the war on terror on 7 October 2001. It was a war based on a convenient myth of Afghan responsibility for 9/11. The real Afghanistan of the young shepherd boys, village wedding parties, grandmothers and babies, killed by US bombs, was invisible and dehumanised in a decade of its people being used for deadly experiments in enforcing Western power. Similarly, the devastated individual families in this book have been invisible here, mostly in Britain, dehumanised and expendable in cruel experiments in social control, which left some dead, others mentally or physically broken. Authorities at every level of government, the legal system and the media have failed to see beyond myths of terrorist threats triggered by stereotypes of oppressed, angry or passive women, unknowable behind a black veil. Prejudice and manufactured fear has fed the cruelty and stupidity of the war on terror and scarred and changed British society itself.

Nothing has been changed more than Afghanistan ten years after the 2001 attack and the ambitious goal of President George W. Bush and Prime Minister Tony Blair of re-making it into a different country. In 2012 the US was preparing for peace talks with a section of the Taliban, accelerating troop withdrawals from the quagmire of its 450 bases in the country and spending $11 billion a year solely on training Afghanistan's own security forces. But at the same time, looking to the future shape of this unfinished US war, tens of millions of dollars were being poured into nearly 130 projects in Herat, Helmand and Kandahar for giant bases with clandestine drone facilities and a new special forces compound for black capture/kill operations.[2]

Afghanistan is just one element of the vast scope of the so-called war on terror, which in fact long pre-dated that coinage by President Bush after 9/11. It had its roots in decades of Western alliances with corrupt and repressive regimes across the Middle East and beyond. The key ones for this book are Egypt and Jordan, while Algeria, Libya, Iraq, Saudi Arabia and Pakistan are also in the picture. The distortion of the politics and economies of their societies was to a great extent a by-product of decades of Western policy in the post-colonial world. In 2011 much of this house of cards collapsed, in the idealism, bravery and power struggles of the Arab Spring in Tunisia and Egypt. The impact of the Arab Spring on some of the women in this book was an explosion of new dreams – of going home, of going to live in an Arab country or just of seeing a husband outside a prison visiting room. For others it was too late.

Egypt was the natural fulcrum of the 2011 upheaval. During the Arab nationalist heyday of Gamal Abdel Nasser in the new Republic of Egypt 60 years before, his imprisoning and torture of Islamists who had been his early allies cast a shadow over his, and Egypt's, pre-eminence in the Middle East. After Nasser's death in 1970 his successor, President Anwar Sadat, soon lost that pre-eminence and greatly increased the regime's trial of strength with the Muslim Brotherhood and other opposition groups in Egypt, by transforming his country into a key US ally and recipient of massive US aid – much of it military.

Sadat's decision to make peace with Israel, with the first visit to Israel by an Arab leader in 1977, the Camp David negotiations of 1978 and the opening of full diplomatic relations with Israel in 1980, cut Egypt off from the rest of the Middle East. And cut the regime off from its people. The Arab summit in Khartoum in 1967, in the wake of the June Arab/Israeli war, which so scarred the Arab world, had declared: no recognition of the Jewish state, no negotiations, no peace treaties. Except for Egypt, the Arab regimes stuck to it. For the Arab street then it was an unchallengeable act of faith to stand for Palestinian rights.

The Egyptian regime's consequent political isolation in the Middle East was particularly striking against the background of the momentous upheaval elsewhere in the Muslim world in 1979. A key pole of American, British and Israeli interests in the region collapsed with the popular revolution against another long-standing US strategic ally, the Shah of Iran, and his replacement by an Islamic state. Just such an Islamic state was the dream that half a century before lay behind the creation of the Muslim Brotherhood in Egypt by Hassan al-Banna. The Iranian revolution of 1979 electrified the whole of the Muslim world and was a major strategic and political setback for the West.[3]

Less than two years later, the US was humiliated again in Iran with the abortive US raid in the summer of 1980 to rescue 52 US hostages held in the Tehran embassy. President Sadat allowed Egypt to be used as the springboard for this initiative. It was a decision that enraged his own people and further deepened his international isolation – except from the US.[4]

That same year, the US under President Jimmy Carter was setting in motion a strategic initiative which dwarfed events in Iran – the drawing of the Soviet Union into what his security adviser, Zbigniew Brzezinski, called 'giving the USSR it's Vietnam war'. The US began secret funding of the *mujahedeen* fighters against the pro-Soviet, nationalist government in Kabul.[5] Six months later the Soviets fell into 'the Afghan trap' and entered Afghanistan for the nearly ten years of war, which combined with internal factors to contribute to the break-up of the Soviet Union.

To the US administration, that secret funding had been 'an excellent idea'. For the national security adviser, looking back 20 years later, there were no regrets. 'What is most important to the history of the world? The Taliban, or the collapse of the Soviet empire? Some stirred-up Muslims or the liberation of Central Europe and the end of the Cold War?'[6] Brzezinski's throw-away line completely under-estimated the impact of the decision he had been part of in entering Afghanistan's civil war. In fact the blow-back it would bring to the US was not far in the future as he spoke.

The response to the Soviet invasion of Afghanistan in December 1979 was that tens of thousands of Muslims, bankrolled by the US and Saudi Arabia, were drawn into a religious war in East Asia. This migration of men and their families from a great variety of countries started another thread of this story of the war on terror, and had a direct effect on many of the families in this book. And in particular, the women from Chapters 1, 2 and 4 were part of this migration. Sabah taught at an international school in Pakistan and was deeply happy, Zinnira looked after her babies in Afghanistan, while Hamda described her time living in Pakistan as, 'sitting on hot coals all the time – I couldn't wait for him to finish so we could get home to Jordan'.[7]

For decades, the Cold War and the perceived threat of nuclear war with the Soviet Union had held US governments, and their people, in thrall to the fear of communism. Part of the

US response to a perceived spread of communism was secretly funded wars, using proxies – just as with the *mujahedeen* in Afghanistan – in South and Central America and in Southern Africa.[8] As in Afghanistan, the US attempted to contain nationalist movements – allied with Cuba or the Soviet Union. The results in countries such as Angola and El Salvador were utterly devastating, as in Afghanistan a few years later.

Yet in that different media age these were largely invisible wars, and they had little or no echo beyond their geographic area. Those US wars, which for those who saw them close up seemed ambitious attempts to change the character of the society at the time, are dwarfed by the scale of death and destruction that has grown out of just one of them today – Afghanistan. And touching the emotions of the billion and a half followers of the world's largest religion produced something on another scale entirely.

In a decade the anti-Soviet *jihad* in Afghanistan transformed to an anti-Saudi *jihad*, and then to an anti-American *jihad*. The defeat and humiliation of one superpower fired many of the individual foot-soldiers involved to believe the second could be similarly vulnerable. The end of the Soviet/Afghan war meant that the US lost interest in the area, the government of Pakistan no longer wanted tens of thousands of Arabs and other foreign Muslims on its soil, and the great majority set off back home. The *jihad* soon had a dozen faces.

That moment of the early 1990s saw the Middle East transformed by acute tension over the first Gulf War as the US sought Middle East allies for its coalition to attack Saddam Hussein in Iraq with Operation Desert Storm, which was deeply unpopular in much of the region. Returnees from the Afghan war were looked on with suspicion by the Westernised regimes of a number of Middle East and North African countries, especially those allied to the US, and several of the families in this book were among those who successfully sought asylum in Britain. Dina told me, 'We left in a hurry, everyone did, suddenly the Pakistan government was having a problem with Arab people ... I don't even know why we came here to England, my husband never discussed it with me. I suppose it was because his friends were coming.'[9]

Meanwhile, in the 1990s, local wars in Algeria, Bosnia and Chechnya involved a jigsaw that included many fighters who had been in Afghanistan. All of these wars, however different politically, also had a profound wake-up effect on many other far away Muslim communities – in Britain for one. Twenty years on, across a wide political spectrum, British Muslims, who had been in their teens and twenties, would say unhesitatingly that Bosnia changed their lives. Bosnian fighters visited Britain, spoke eloquently in mosques and universities of how much they needed help against the Serb war machine's brutal power.

Young Muslims were horrified and moved to action by films of atrocities and by the stories of Bosnian refugees who were sheltered in many British mosques.[10] Some young men drove aid convoys, some enlisted as fighters. This part of their lives would later, after 9/11 2001 in New York or 7/7 2005 in London, make some of them targets of the vast US intelligence fishing net, which saw Bosnia's foreign sympathisers as linked to Al Qaeda and a danger to the US. But nothing illustrated this more graphically than the fate of the six Algerian/Bosnians, then settled in the fragile post-war Bosnian state, who were rendered by the US to Guantanamo Bay prison, after flimsy charges of plotting to attack the US and British embassies in Sarajevo had been dismissed by the Bosnian courts. The 'plot' evaporated and the six men found themselves being interrogated for years about Arabs and other foreign Muslims, who might have had links to Al Qaeda, in Bosnia during the war in which the US had given tacit support to Bosnia against the Serbs.[11] One such man was Babar Ahmed from South London whom many men from Britain in Guantanamo were questioned about (see Chapter 6).

In the 1930s, hundreds of young British men and women from a variety of leftist backgrounds went to volunteer in the

International Brigades as fighters, medics or aid workers, in defence of the Spanish Republican government. They were moved, like the young foreign Muslims in Bosnia, by a mixture of political and human solidarity instincts. The experience changed their lives. Forty years later, thousands more British men and women were involved for decades in supporting the liberation wars in Southern Africa. A small number, mainly young communists, from Britain were recruited by the exiled African National Congress and South African Communist Party leadership for clandestine propaganda and underground resistance work inside apartheid South Africa.[12] None of these war zones, though, had the extra dynamic – which made Bosnia and then Chechnya and then Afghanistan such a magnet – of it being a requirement of their faith to support other Muslims under threat.

In Algeria in 1991, an ossified single party state, which had grown out of the liberation war against France, unexpectedly faced losing power to an Islamist party in elections. It could perhaps have been predicted, with the death in 1978 of President Houari Boumediene, the subsequent loss of authority by the party, its corruption and blatant privileges, the changes in the constitution in the 1980s, plus the unsolved structural problems of the economy making everyday life increasingly difficult. For the ten years before, at least, a time bomb of unemployed youth, disadvantaged by a badly managed and abrupt change from French to Arabic in education, was getting ready to explode. The elections were cancelled, a military government took over, thousands of supporters of the Islamist party disappeared into prison camps in the Sahara, and a civil war with splintering opposition groups and black operations by the government brought untold suffering to Algerians, especially in the rural areas.[13]

Young Algerian men fled for safety to Europe, including Britain, in droves in the mid-1990s, believing they could not make a life in Algeria. Some of them went to live in Afghanistan during those years, seeing it, under the Taliban, as a young

Islamic country, where they could make a contribution with their education and skills, and a place that seemed to offer a more peaceful civilian life than what they had fled from. 'Afghanistan seemed like Utopia – it was the most beautiful place I ever saw, when I woke the first morning after crossing the border at night', one man who made that choice explained many years later, when he was living in Britain on deportation bail, with a 22-hour curfew, after spending seven years in UK prisons on secret evidence, without a trial (see Chapter 8).

Another focus of the time was Chechnya's two wars for independence from Russia where half a million people were displaced, unknown tens of thousands killed and the capital Grozny flattened in 1995. These were David and Goliath struggles between Islam and a communist regime, which attracted some of those who had fought the Soviets in Afghanistan, and many others who had seen that war up close or been deeply stirred by Bosnia. London became a hub of support for the little-known Chechen resistance against Russia (see Chapter 6).

Somewhat aside from active solidarity in these wars was a sophisticated Muslim intellectual world of struggle. London was already 'a hub of sorts for Islamist politics in the 1990s ... the dominant image of political Islam was the bloody record of the Egyptian insurgency, the Algerian civil war and the ascent of Mr Bin Laden ... but no less seismic was the shift underway within currents inspired by the Muslim Brotherhood'.[14] The *New York Times* reporter, Anthony Shadid, traced this story of political Islam's evolution in Britain in a key decade, in a series of interviews with the exiled Tunisian Said Ferjani, who was one of many who returned in 2011 after 20 years in London. Most important was the influence of the exiled Tunisian leader, Sheikh Rashid Ghannouchi, who had concluded – since before his first imprisonment by President Bourgiba in the 1980s and based on his own *shariah* studies – that for Islamists to work with other groups such as social democrats or leftist trade unions was correct. The Algerian Islamists followed him with their participation in the 1991 elections, which they won and had stolen. But they then moved away from his line into the civil war following, as he put it, 'the punishment of the Islamic victors in the Tunisian and Algerian elections'. Tunisia's En Nahdha party, however, maintained Ghannouchi's liberal path despite their election also being hijacked and followed by torture, killings, repression and arrests.[15]

Back in Afghanistan, what Anthony Shadid called 'the Manichean view of the world of Mr Bin Laden'[16] produced a piece of paper that changed history. In Osama Bin Laden's camp in February 1998, a declaration of an 'International Islamic Front for Jihad against Jews and Crusaders' was signed by Mr Bin Laden, individually, not in the name of Al Qaeda, and by his Egyptian ally, Ayman Zawahiri, also as an individual.

The group that would become Al Qaeda had had some stunning early failures. The 1993 New York bombing of the World Trade Center, which killed six people and injured 100, did not quite have an Al Qaeda address. Although its authors included Ramzi Yousef, the nephew of Al Qaeda's Khalid Sheikh Mohammed, Yousef was not, according to his uncle later, an Al Qaeda member, and the others involved were more prominently linked to Egyptian Islamic Jihad (EIJ) in the person of the blind Sheikh Omar Abdel-Rahman. Then there was the first airline plot 'Bojinka', hatched in Asia by Ramzi Yousef and his uncle.[17] It would have used ten planes with explosives left on board by the bombers who would themselves leave the planes during stop-overs on flights from Asia to the US. The plot was discovered by a chance fire in an apartment during bomb making preparations in 1995.

The US embassy bombings in East Africa in the summer of 1998 were the devastating successful opening move by Al Qaeda, which would lead to 9/11. More than 200 people were killed, including 12 Americans in Nairobi, in an attack timed for the eighth anniversary of the arrival of US troops in Saudi Arabia – one of the key US strategic decisions that set Bin Laden on his course.

In retaliation for the embassy bombings the US bombed targets in both Sudan and Afghanistan, though they were not, as it turned out, Al Qaeda targets. Eighteen months later 17 American servicemen were killed and 40 wounded in an Al Qaeda attack on the USS Cole in harbour in Aden – a suicide attack from a small boat, which blew a 30-foot by 30-foot hole in the ship, organised by Abd al Rahim al Nashiri.[18] That attack, like many of the pre-9/11 attacks, was conducted from Yemen, which, like Somalia, was seen by Al Qaeda as the strategic key to choking Western supply lines to Afghanistan.[19]

The key architects of that written pact of 1998 in Afghanistan came out of the very different worlds of opposition politics in Egypt and a life of ease in Saudi Arabia. Ayman Zawahiri was scarred by one of the harshest of political experiences in the Middle East. He was a veteran of years of prisons and torture, under the regime of Sadat, and then of President Hosni Mubarak after Sadat's assassination in 1981. He left Egypt to work as a doctor in Saudi Arabia. He then became a close associate of Bin Laden, the soft spoken, millionaire Saudi, product of a Jeddah elite private school with British teachers, where he became part of an after-school Islamic group run by an exiled Syrian PE teacher with Muslim Brotherhood ideas.[20] Zawahiri would later have a price on his head of $25 million.

Zawahiri brought to Afghanistan the factionalised and secretive world of Egyptian Islamic opposition politics in the 1970s, 1980s and 1990s. Offshoots of the 50-year-old Muslim Brotherhood – a legitimate non-violent opposition party – the Islamic Group (IG) and EIJ sought the violent overthrow of Sadat and Mubarak's governments. Like the Muslim Brotherhood leaders and tens of thousands of its activists, these small groups' members paid a horrendous price of years of torture and imprisonment. They were composed of cells of highly educated professionals – doctors, engineers, soldiers and lawyers, like Zawahiri and Adel Abdul Bary. The Egyptians' own organisations had had more than 20 years of life in political struggle before Al Qaeda was born, and were built on half a century of the Muslim Brotherhood culture of political Islam.

However, by the mid-1990s EIJ and IG had been broken inside Egypt, and many members were in prison or in exile, like the lawyer Adel Abdul Bary, whose wife, Ragaa, had found her first years of happiness in her marriage in a country, Britain, where she could not speak the language (see Chapter 5).

A number of individuals from these organisations were with Zawahiri in the Bin Laden entourage in Peshawar, then in Sudan, then in Afghanistan. Zawahiri's signing of the 1998 document produced furious email exchanges and declarations denouncing him, by EIJ members and former members. It took EIJ far away from their goal of political change in Egypt, and into Bin Laden's wholly different area of targeting US interests. The IG leader, Rifai Taha, was forced by his members to withdraw his signature.[21]

The thinking behind the 1998 declaration of global *jihad* against the US and its allies was a miscalculation with fatal consequences for Muslim countries such as Afghanistan and Iraq, Pakistan and Yemen, and countless individual Muslims, on a scale of destruction few foresaw. The Abdul Bary family's peaceful life in London was one Egyptian casualty that illustrates how far the collateral damage struck, when the US targeted him for extradition as they lumped together Al Qaeda and EIJ/IG.

The massive case of *USA* v. *Usama Bin Laden et al.* – and Abdul Bary's extradition case of 1999 – depended on the anonymous testimony of a man called 'Confidential Source number 1' – the first Al Qaeda traitor, described as the Rosetta Stone by US investigators. But years later the man emerged as a Sudanese, Jamal Ahmed al Fadl.[22] He appeared in court as a witness against other people, was much written about, and there were many questions about how knowledgeable he really was about Al Qaeda's affairs. He certainly left because he stole $110,000, which Bin Laden told him to return.[23] He never met Abdul Bary, nor mentioned him in his evidence about the supposed organisational link between Al Qaeda and the Egyptian Islamist groups. The US prosecutors, however, used this to implicate automatically individual members or ex-members without any proven link between the individuals concerned.

Al Fadl's new life in a witness protection programme in the US, with his family brought over from Sudan, cost the US taxpayer millions of dollars and used countless hours, weeks and months of the lives of the FBI minders who took care of him over several years and gave him the nickname 'Junior' due to his adolescent behaviour. Besides the lack of credibility of this sole witness, there were serious questions over the conduct of the prosecutors. Long after the initial case began, it emerged that 18 video-conferences between Al Fadl and New York prosecutors were taped, and lawyers maintained that they showed Al Fadl being moulded and manipulated. All this was withheld from the defence team and British officials.

One man who, back in 2001, did make just such a forecast of disaster for his own country from Bin Laden's actions was Abdul Salam Zaeef, Taliban ambassador to Pakistan, who wept when he saw the Al Qaeda attack that made the Twin Towers fall in 2001. He made the parallel with the US use of nuclear bombs on Japan in retaliation for Pearl Harbour, and wept for the disaster that would befall his country. After consulting with the Taliban leader, Mullah Omar, by telephone, Zaeef dictated the Taliban press release condemning 9/11 and saying those responsible should be brought to justice.[24] The offer was ignored and Zaeef spent four years in prison in Guantanamo Bay, before he wrote his book of memoirs, translated from Pashto.

The attack of 9/11 came on the watch of one of the most ideological of teams ever in the White House. And President Bush himself had close relations with a British Prime Minister equally ready to see the response to terrorist attacks not in terms of preparing court cases, but in terms of his and Bush's personal responsibility to launch a revenge war. As Bush put it, 'our war on terror begins with Al Qaeda, but it does not end there. It will not end until every terrorist group of global reach has been found, stopped and defeated ... Americans should not expect one battle, but a lengthy campaign, unlike any other we have seen.'[25]

Already, in 1996, President Bill Clinton had urged the passage of the Antiterrorism and Effective Death Penalty Act, which foreshadowed post 9/11 legislation such as the USA PATRIOT Act. Although its genesis was the 1995 Oklahoma City bombing carried out by Timothy McVeigh, in fact only people of Arab descent were subjected to the secret detention provision of the act.[26]

After 9/11, Blair and Bush stoked fear in their core constituencies at home and launched what was effectively an anti-Muslim crusade, at home as well as abroad. The PATRIOT Act and subsequent legislation gave the US government extraordinarily wide powers including the Attorney General's right to arrest, indefinitely detain or deport anyone, even if they had committed no crime, massive surveillance of mosques and Muslim Americans, a new regime of selective enforcement of immigration laws, prohibition of legal and other 'material support' to a wide number of groups deemed 'terrorist', and data mining on a massive scale. Guantanamo was the centrepiece of the reaction to 9/11, and remains the symbol of how half a century of international conventions on torture, prisoners' rights, rendition and other aspects of international law were simply over-ridden by the US government and its allies.

This was the context in which in the US after 9/11 at least 1200 people, mostly Arab, South Asian and Muslim citizens and non-citizens, were arrested, often held in solitary confinement and many deported, although not one of them was ever linked to the events of 9/11.[27]

In a vast fishing expedition across the Middle East, Pakistan and Afghanistan, and from Bosnia to Gambia, thousands more – many of them entirely innocent – were captured or turned in for $5,000 bounties. The Geneva Conventions were set aside, and the men were detained in Kandahar, Bagram and, from 11 January 2002, in Guantanamo Bay in Cuba. Here they were held beyond the reach of US law, without *habeas corpus*, in conditions that were flagrant violations of international law. Torture was widely and systematically practiced, as men were subjected to clandestine rendition flights to secret CIA-run prisons in Europe and Asia, or sent to be tortured in prisons from Morocco to Syria or Egypt.[28]

Back home in London, wives like Sabah (see Chapter 1) were tortured themselves through sleepless nights. She had no word from her husband from Guantanamo for three years to set against the images and reports of torture of the imprisoned men, which first came as whispers, but then as such a television constant that she stopped watching news programmes. And Amani, whose brother was with Sabah's husband in Guantanamo, suffered devastating flashes of picturing him after the family got the first news, from a lawyer, of the injuries he had sustained in prison. 'I was overwhelmed by it all', she said many years later.

The months and years in Guantanamo of repetitive interrogation of men, stripped naked in front of females, held in freezing containers, kept awake for as long as 20 hours a day for at least two months,[29] were military intelligence gathering based on the 'mosaic' theory of gradually building an intelligence picture of Al Qaeda and its support base. The Bush Administration first articulated the 'mosaic' theory within days of 9/11.[30]

In Britain, as around the world, the security services worked closely with their US colleagues (see Chapter 1, for their visit to Sabah's house, and Chapter 6) in the fishing net that captured men who would spend years in Guantanamo or in other prisons in the UK. A new anti-terrorism law was rushed through Parliament in late 2011, including the provision that the Home Secretary could detain indefinitely without trial foreign men suspected of being linked to terrorism, but who could not be deported to their home countries because they could face torture, or worse. The evidence against them was held in secret[31] (see Josephine, Dina and Hamda in Chapters 3 and 4). The dozen Muslim Arab men first arrested and held in Belmarsh prison soon called it Britain's Guantanamo.

The Wikileaks Guantanamo files would underline how slight the 'evidence' was against many of the men in Guantanamo, the vast majority of whom were held but never charged with a crime. The supposed intelligence compiled against them was thoroughly infected with the unreliable testimony of tortured, coerced and bribed prisoners.[32]

Years of academic research in the Department of Defense's own papers, by a US-based Seton Hall Law School team under Professor Mark Denbeaux, revealed not only who the prisoners were, but that the US administration knew they had largely innocent men even while they were describing them as the 'worst of the worst'. Denbeaux and his team produced exhaustive research on the lawlessness of Guantanamo, including particular horrors such as the grim obfuscated circumstances in which the young Saudi, Yasser al Zahrani, and two others, who were officially described as suicides 'conducting asymmetrical warfare', actually died.[33] (The film, *Death in Guantanamo*, four years in the making by the Norwegian journalist Erling Borgen, tells this story in the words of Yasser's family, as well as the men who were his colleagues in Guantanamo.)

The Seton Hall research demolished the Bush administration's well-honed myths about Guantanamo in a testimony to the Senate Armed Services Committee. 'Remarkably, 66% of those detained at Guantanamo were *not* captured in Afghanistan, much less on the battlefield. Rather, this group was handed over to the United States by Pakistan. Another 20% were delivered to the US by the Northern Alliance.' Other Seton Hall statistics showed that more than 55 per cent of those detained in Guantanamo were *not* accused of ever having committed a single hostile act against the United States or its coalition; only 8 per cent of the detainees were characterised by the Department of Defense as 'al Qaeda fighters'; of the remaining detainees, 40 per cent had no definitive connection with Al Qaeda at all and 18 per cent had no definitive affiliation with either Al Qaeda or the Taliban. (And the Taliban government of Afghanistan had never declared itself at war with the United States, but rather was the recipient of a US bombing campaign and an extensive military operation for regime change after 9/11, even as they sought a trial for Bin Laden in an international arena.)[34] Professor Denbeaux went on to say that the reality was that a very large fraction of the detainees seemed to be, at most, a ragtag collection of 'support' personnel for low-level foot soldiers.[35]

Yet all this available information made no impact against the steamroller of propaganda about the men in Guantanamo from the US and UK governments and their media allies, which had implanted fear of Muslims and continued to stoke it. Guantanamo, like the torture practices at Abu Ghraib prison in Iraq, was a demonstration of power to America's enemies, and a demonstration to its own people of America's commitment to their security.

Within days of Guantanamo Bay prison opening in Cuba in January 2002, lawyers from the Centre for Constitutional Rights (CCR) in New York began gathering a legal team to challenge it. The president of CCR, Michael Ratner, said much later:

> Immediately after 9/11 we saw the round up of Muslims in the US, accused of terrorism though in fact, if anything, they had minor registration issues, and the FBI deciding to visit 5,000 young Muslim men. There was a mood of incredible animosity. In this atmosphere, and with these terrible legal precedents, we never expected we had any chance to win anything on Guantanamo. In fact it looked totally impossible ... we were tilting at windmills.[36]

Despite a stunning success in a Supreme Court judgment in 2004, granting the right to access to US courts, years later many of the finest minds in the US legal system were still unable to get any legal recourse for their Guantanamo clients in lengthy appeals battles through levels of courts, with a US judiciary honed by ideology to support the US President's personal exceptional powers.[37]

Michael Ratner pin-pointed the worst moment for the lawyers' fraternity as when President Obama refused entry to the US from Guantanamo of 17 ethnic Chinese Muslim Uighers, despite a federal court order and despite there being 300 Uighers in Washington ready to host them. 'Our hopes were just unravelling.'

On 14 September 2011 Congress had authorised the President to use military force against Al Qaeda, giving him, as commander in chief, the exceptional wartime powers he would not have had in peacetime. One of those lawyers who fought case after case against the Bush administration's detentions called those Washington years a time of 'imperial power', and forecast that Guantanamo's lasting damage had been to the US Constitution, to the country and to the rule of law.[38]

Michael Ratner spoke of the Obama years as, 'Presidential power supreme – Guantanamo, Bagram, indefinite detention, wars in country after country. Obama actually entrenched all the Bush era bad stuff – except only water-boarding ...'

A general manufactured climate of fear of Arabs and Muslims, in the US in particular, was already a well-known phenomenon before all this, often linked to efficient and well-funded pro-Israel lobbyists.[39] That climate was further stoked by Western governments and media after the shock of 9/11, and there was little protest on behalf of these Guantanamo prisoners – anonymous Muslims who few people in the West knew and who were branded as terrorists. As the years went by, and the level of fear remained constantly high, fed by a steady trickle of arrests of people said to be terrorists, many of them within the United States, Guantanamo and its lawlessness came to be tolerated, and even openly praised by some US media and politicians, and broadly accepted as the price of security.

In the US a number of landmark 'material support' cases saw American Muslim men with no accusation of direct funding of terrorism sentenced to long prison terms. It took the government two trials to convict Ghassan Elashi and Shukri Abu Baker, chair and chief executive of the US's largest Muslim charity, the Texas-based Holy Land Foundation. They were sentenced to 65 years in jail for sending $12.4 million to charitable 'Zakat committees' in Gaza, which were not on any government terrorism list, but which the prosecution said were fronts for Hamas. The funds had been earmarked for orphanages and community welfare groups. Unsuccessful legal attempts to appeal the cases showed the 'equation of Islamist social institutions with violence ... a guise for promoting terrorism ... deeply embedded and uncritically embraced at many levels of US society including the Supreme Court'.[40]

In another similar case, Sami Al Arian, a professor of engineering at the University of South Florida and outspoken campaigner for Palestinian rights, was indicted in 2003 on multiple counts of 'material support for terrorism'. In a 2006 trial, after nearly three years in solitary confinement, the jury acquitted him on half of the charges, while they were deadlocked on the others, with ten jurors to two wanting to acquit. He took a plea bargain on one count, agreed to deportation and should have been freed the following year. But he was then charged with criminal contempt when he would not testify in another trial. In 2009 he was released to house arrest, where in three years he was allowed to leave his apartment twice – for his daughters' weddings (see Chapters 7 and 8).

In 2003 an Iraqi-American oncologist, Dr Rafil Dhafir, was characterised as a terrorist by Attorney General John Ashcroft, and later sentenced to 22 years in prison for violating Iraqi sanctions by sending food and medicine to meet the widely recognised humanitarian catastrophe in his country of birth, through a charity, Help the Needy, which was not properly registered. He was resentenced in 2012 to the same period.

The 86-year sentence given in 2010 to the Pakistani neuro-scientist Dr Aafia Siddiqui – kidnapped with her three children and disappeared for years – for attempted murder of US officials, was another marker of the judiciary's extreme politicisation. And the unanimous guilty verdict against her by a New York jury, despite the lack of forensic evidence to back the stories of the serving soldiers who testified against her, was a marker of media and public opinion attitudes. In all these cases, while terrorist accusations were freely and repeatedly made publicly against them, no terrorist accusations were ever brought into the court cases.

By October 2011 the US had convicted 362 people in terrorism cases, of which 269 were connected to international terrorism. They included nationals and non-nationals, many whose sentences were reduced after they cooperated and named other men, many who were arrested after official US sting operations. One such case was Amadullah Niazi, reportedly the brother-in-law of Bin Laden's bodyguard, accused to planning terror attacks in California, whose case collapsed in September 2010 when it emerged that he had been enticed and entrapped by a former criminal working for the FBI, and had reported the man to his local mosque as a dangerous extremist. Craig Monteilh, also known as Farouk Al Aziz between July 2006 and October 2007, was paid $200,000 to infiltrate mosques in California and record conversations for the FBI.[41] Another such case was Amine el-Khalifi, arrested in Washington in early 2012 and accused of wearing a suicide vest (which had no suicide material in it) sold to him by an FBI agent.

Many of the convicted men were held in solitary confinement in a highly restricted SuperMax prison even while awaiting trial or preparing plea bargains, and later in special Communications Management Units (CMUs) inhabited mainly by Muslims, which were created in 2006 and 2008 at Terre Haute, Indiana, and Marion, Illinois. They are dehumanising regimes, with no physical contact allowed with visitors and restrictions and monitoring of mail and phone contacts. (Noor Elaishy was one daughter who transformed her young student life, dedicating herself to see that her father would not serve 65 years in prison; see Chapter 7.)

In Britain post 9/11, fear of Muslims and routine Islamophobia in the media were prevalent through the following decade. Prime Minister Blair's confident world view of Al Qaeda sympathisers being in every group of Muslim dissidents, from a wide range of countries, prevailed in British foreign and domestic policy over any more nuanced information he was given.[42]

In fact the most serious terrorist attack in Britain was by young British men opposed to UK policy in Iraq, Afghanistan and Palestine. It hit London in July 2005, traumatising the country. Two weeks later, a similar plot by a group of UK residents from the Horn of Africa failed, and those concerned received long prison sentences. A 2006 airline plot with echoes of Al Qaeda's 'Bojinka' plot, seemingly an era away, similarly failed and brought long sentences to its authors. A host of smaller suspected terrorism cases were brought to trial, often to be thrown out by juries, such as one involving a young woman who wrote poetry that was deemed by the government to serve terrorist objectives. And a university student, who was arrested after he had a friend download Al Qaeda material for his thesis, received hefty damages from the police. There was also the notorious Ricin plot, which sent a number of Algerian men to prison to await a lengthy trial that ended with acquittals and the discovery that there was no Ricin and no plot.

The story of what happened to a number of Muslim families in Britain in the decade-long fallout from 9/11 is a microcosm of this big picture of fear, which spawned Islamophobia and systematised injustice. By knowing something of who these families were, and are, and what are the hinterlands of their lives, the reader can break through the stereotypes that made them only the shadowy 'other'. These experiences throw into sharp relief the way our own society has developed deviant and authoritarian trends, and a prison policy for Muslims based on a dehumanising cruelty. Through these women's experiences emerges the normalisation of new forms of torture and cruel and degrading treatment: an extension of prison to home.

Almost all of the women in this book are my friends, several of them for half a dozen years or more. I came to know them by chance, after one friendship led slowly to another. In the early years it was a steep learning curve for me to spend time in homes where faith was the primary reality, English was the second language, and privacy and reticence were the marked characteristics. I never intended to write about them and was for a long time incapable of finding words for so much I never knew about, that went on so near to home. I had found a world in Britain that I did not recognise.

For those living under Control Orders it meant getting cleared by the Home Office for visits to their houses, while visits to Category A prisoners in high security prisons meant police and intelligence service clearance after home visits, and having to sign a statement that I would not write about the prison and my visits.

Beyond those hurdles, I found in the fabric of these families' every day experience a series of hard culture shocks. I found, for instance, women who had suffered complete mental breakdowns being looked after with loving care by husbands who could only step outside for very restricted hours. I found women in Control Order families coping with children's needs for a normal life, against a background of acute stress, depression and suicide attempts, with almost no network able to help.

In these homes over the months and years I began to see grief, impotence and despair close up, and more painful to relate to than that of the many thousands of refugee women, war victims and orphans whose lives I had spent 40 years reporting, from places such as Vietnam, Cambodia, Angola, Mozambique, Uganda, Somalia, Liberia, Eritrea, Palestine, Colombia and other places crippled by war and poverty.

So much was invisible, like the smiling man living on a 24-hour a day curfew, or the pain of lonely young women whose husbands were on UN asset freezing sanctions and could not touch money, leaving the wife, with her small children, obliged to do all shopping and to show every receipt for every pencil, bottle of milk or washing up liquid to the Home Office every month. It was a Kafka world where accepting a lift or a present could be judged by the Home Office as a breach of the family's conditions, which could trigger a prison sentence. Families broke up. Impeccable neat homes, where Arabic calligraphy from the Koran was the only ornament, and television was barred as a bad influence, were lost overnight. Children got sick, with nightmares and anxiety attacks, or were bullied in school. Careers were abruptly at an end. Men came back from prison very changed, 'You have to be very careful how you speak to these men – they've survived traumas they don't even tell about ... I see my husband struggling. The kids are struggling. It's hard ... it's hard, every single day.' Incredible resilience and sacrifice carried women and their families through experiences of humiliation and isolation. Several of these women became the one resource of understanding for other women who hit despair.

A regime of isolation and cruelty to whole families has been, effectively, an experiment carried out mainly on foreigners, and entirely on Muslims – several have gone mad, others just kept going by the care of other prisoners, or random acts of kindness from strangers.

Among the Muslim community in Britain, especially the young, there was general knowledge of some of these cases, and the mainstream indifference to them was, like Britain's foreign policy through the years of the Iraq and Afghan wars and the sharply deteriorating situation of Palestinians, key to the barely contained anger of some of this Muslim generation, which was one of the fault-lines in our society.

It has been a long journey from the intellectual and political home I had for years on the edge of the secular world of

African liberation movements, and the wars against them funded from Washington and Pretoria, which caused so much death, destruction and hunger in the 1970s and 1980s. That was another closed and embattled world, a sideshow of the Cold War. But it was a clearly defined struggle for political and economic power, focused between Western support for the survival of the apartheid regime in South Africa, and Cuban and Soviet support for nationalist movements, usually wrongly dubbed communist. That world had coherence and logic – both markedly absent in the great Western intelligence fishing net for President Bush's 'mosaic', which had gathered up and tortured men from the families I began to know. It took me a long time to understand quite how absent.

After a decade, the horror of what happened, and is still happening, to countries, and to individuals like these, in the name of US and UK national security, has faded for most of the general public. The enormity of the injustice perpetrated over a decade and more has been airbrushed out of mainstream America's and Britain's consciousness. How did we get so coarsened that this is virtually unremarked? The war on terror has been successful in winning so many people over to accepting that the abuse of a few is justified in the name of protecting the many.

'It is unbelievable ... there has been not a ripple of outrage ... I thought people would rise up ... John was photographed, bound, naked in the winter, by US troops', commented Frank Lindh, father of the young Californian student of Islam, John Walker Lindh.[43] John was given a 20-year sentence in a plea bargain, after being nearly killed during a massacre by US allies in Afghanistan. He is serving it in the CMU in Terre Haute, Indiana, where all visits are with a glass partition keeping his parents from touching him.

1
Sabah: From Palestine to Guantanamo

'Allah will never give me more pain than I can bear.'

In the spring of 2004, preparing the programme notes for the Tricycle Theatre's production of the verbatim play, *Guantanamo, Honour Bound to Defend Freedom*, I came across a letter written by a child from one of the families that had not wanted to be interviewed for the play, and which I had therefore been curious about. I wondered who they were and how they fitted into the jigsaw of men from Britain who had ended up in Guantanamo, and whose stories were in the play as small vignettes, unconnected to their real full lives. This family did not even have that small mark in the outside world.

The father of the child, Jamil el Banna, had been arrested in Banjul in West Africa by the Gambian intelligence services, accompanied by Americans, with his best friend, an Iraqi also living in the UK named Bisher al Rawi. An interview for the play with Bisher's brother Wahab (who had been arrested too and then released as he had a British passport whereas the others were UK residents, not citizens) had produced a story utterly incomprehensible to me. One line stuck in my mind. Wahab described asking his guards and interrogators, who included two Americans, to see the British High Commissioner, and being told that the High Commissioner didn't want to see him. His captors went on, 'who do you think ordered your arrest? The British already knew you were in this situation.'

Anas el Banna had written his letter a year before I saw it, to Prince Charles, and to the Prime Minister, asking for help to get his father home.

Dear Sir Tony Blair, I am a boy, I am seven years old ...
writing to you this letter from my heart because I miss my
father. I am wishing that you can help me and my father?
I am always asking mother when will he come back? And
my mother says I don't know. Now I have started to know
that my father is in prison in a place called Cuba and I don't
know the reason why and I don't know where is Cuba. Every
night I think of my Dad and I cry in a very low voice so
that my mother does not hear and I dream that he is coming
back home, and gives me a big hug. Every Eid I wait for my
father to come back ... I wish you a happy life with your
children in your house.

The Prime Minister's office did not reply, though Prince
Charles's did, with his private secretary writing a kind letter,
saying that unfortunately the prince was not in a position
to intercede.

I wrote to Anas's mother, at the address on his letter, telling
her about the play and our hopes that it might help in a very
small way towards the men from Britain being released from
Guantanamo. The next day I got a phone call in hesitant
English from Sabah, inviting me to visit them. And at the
weekend I set off with a cake and some children's toys and
games, to the household that would change my attitudes and
understanding of more things than I could have dreamed of.

In a small north London suburban street, there was a smiling
Sabah and three rather wary boys aged between seven and
four, a pretty little three-year-old girl with black curls, and
a baby, born after her father disappeared into Guantanamo
after his business trip to Gambia in late 2002. The house was
a jolt back into Palestinian homes I knew in the West Bank
and Gaza, or the camps in Lebanon, with few possessions, a
picture of Mecca on the wall, no sign of consumerism, a ready
plying of visitors with homemade food, and presents of dried
fruit and a pretty little teapot. The children were polite and

shy, then more fluent in Arabic than in English. Their drawings and writing were stuck up on the kitchen walls.

Visitors were rare enough in the household to cause some excitement, and Sabah talked and talked that afternoon, mostly about her mother and five sisters in Jordan, and about her family's original homes in Jerusalem and Hebron. She spoke about her current very isolated life with just two friends in London. She spoke to them only on the phone, as she had done to Jamil's solicitor, Gareth Peirce, in the 18 months since he disappeared.

She also mentioned that before Jamil left they had two visits to their house from Special Branch, one accompanied by an American. My mind briefly replayed Wahab's words. Only later would I understand all this as part of the vast Western intelligence post-9/11 fishing net, which sent so many innocent men like Jamil to Guantanamo. That afternoon I was deeply struck by two things – how much Sabah mentioned Allah and how, amazingly, she seemed to be happy, despite having no way to understand what had happened to her family and missing her husband so much.

At the end she said shyly, 'I'm sorry, I've talked too much.' But it had been far from too much, and I came back often, to sit in the impeccably clean and tidy kitchen, play with the children and look at their homework, and to listen to Sabah talk, about Palestine mostly. In the early months she talked mainly of the past and happiness, and skirted round how she was bearing the frightening unknown behind the long absence of her husband, and the scary sadness in her son's letter to the Prime Minister, showing him trying to shelter his mother from his fears for his Dad. Similarly, Sabah talked about how she tried to shield her own mother in Jordan from knowing what she was feeling, and how on the phone to her she was always bright and optimistic that he would come home soon. It was often so very far from what she felt that desperation would seize her in the night and she would sometimes step outside the house full of sleeping children to cry.

Miraculously she had created a tiny world of happiness and security for her children, although later I would see at what a cost to herself, with her grief for her husband shut tight inside. She said constantly how she referred everything in her life to Allah, 'I can only pray. I know Allah is doing this to me for a reason. Allah knows what is best for me.' Allah was the unseen presence in everything she said, unself-consciously brought into every thought and decision. When an alarm rang in the kitchen for the prayer hour five times a day, she and the children would pray. They all prayed for their Dad, and his friend Bisher (although they didn't know him), to come back from this place called Cuba. Years later the children would ask Sabah hard questions she could not answer about where their father was and why.

Both Sabah and Jamil had known war, exile and separation from family all their lives. Both had been small children when their families fled their homes as the Israeli army occupied Palestinian territory during the 1967 war. They met in Jordan, where she lived with her parents and five sisters and was working as a school-teacher. Jamil had come home then, hoping to get married on a brief visit from Pakistan, where he was teaching Arabic in an orphanage for Afghan children. His mother and sister suggested the young teacher they knew as his bride. 'I told them to be sure to tell him I have one hand that does not work properly, I didn't want him to be disappointed in me when he saw it later', she said.

Sabah herself always wanted to marry a man who was not just an observant Muslim but, 'very special, very pure, very good'. She had been with her mother on the Hajj pilgrimage to Mecca, and Islam was absolutely central to her life. 'I always used to think about Allah and what he would want from me.' She made the decision to wear the scarf when she was fourteen, against her father's advice, as he thought she was too young and would probably change her mind. 'I knew I wouldn't, the *hijab* feels nice.'

A week after they met, they were married, and Sabah went with Jamil to Pakistan – a huge wrench out of her tight-knit family, which she accepted matter-of-factly. Again she taught in a school, this time to children of many nationalities, and the two of them were happily settled there until the US-backed war against the Soviets in Afghanistan came to an abrupt end when the Soviet army withdrew. The Pakistanis then wanted the Arabs living there to leave. Sabah and Jamil, who spoke only minimal words of English, came to London in 1994, following their neighbours and friends from Pakistan – the Palestinian/ Jordanian cleric Mohammed Othman, later known better as Abu Qatada, and his family. (Much later, as he was interrogated and tortured by the Americans, Jamil would realise that this friendship was probably the source of Western intelligence interest in him; see Introduction and Chapter 7.) The couple was granted political asylum in Britain on the basis of Jamil's previous opposition to the Jordanian government. 'He never spoke to me about that, I never knew', Sabah once said.

They lived a very quiet life bringing up their children and seeing little of the British world around them, but keeping in touch mainly with a few Palestinian or other Arab families. In the early days Sabah taught friends' children at home, before they found schools and settled. She never met her husband's new Iraqi friend from the mosque who proposed the business venture in Gambia to him, as a modest woman who did not meet men except family members she only peeped at him from behind a door. Jamil struggled with English, constantly forgetting the new words she taught him, and Gambia probably felt to him the possible opportunity he needed to provide for his family.

The plan was to go to West Africa for a short period and start a mobile peanut oil factory. None of the Arab men involved had experience of anything of the kind, but Wahab put $250,000 of family money into the scheme, the other partners contributed much smaller sums, and by late 2002 they were ready to go.

Sabah had misgivings – only too well-founded, as it turned out – about the planned trip to Africa to launch the project, but she decided to keep them to herself, as a respectful wife. Just before the group was due to leave in November, the police called on her husband. 'We had two visits to the house from police', she recalled, 'once, just after September 11, when there was an American with them, and a woman who spoke Arabic. The second was just before my husband was leaving for Africa. They told Jamil, 'No problem with your visit to Gambia.'

A more worldly person might have seen it as cause for alarm that the authorities already knew of his plans, and worried about leaving the UK armed only with a UN travel document. But in late 2002 probably few people outside the UK intelligence and police circles had any idea of the way Britain in the post-9/11 period had become part of a vast web of data collection on Muslims across the world and their connections to each other. Then Jamil was gone, and the few weeks without her husband became years.

The first British ex-prisoners came back from Guantanamo in the spring of 2004 and that summer, a few months after I first met Sabah, they produced a devastating report for their solicitors about their treatment by the Americans. One Sunday evening I went with her solicitor, Gareth Peirce, to show it to Sabah, and prepare her for the gruesome details of life in Guantanamo from the men who had been alongside her husband, and whose stories would be in the media, including their details of Jamil's very poor health.

A few months before, reports and pictures of torture by Americans of prisoners at Abu Ghraib prison in Iraq had emerged to stun the world with their gross brutality. For Sabah they were a horror she could not get out of her mind. She used to wonder aloud over and over again whether something like this was also happening to Jamil at the hands of the Americans. The only possible answer to this was, 'No, I'm sure it's not the same, Iraq is different.' But now there was no disguising what this legal report reflected of her husband's reality, and there were even grim drawings of the treatment the three young men from Tipton had described. Gareth went through the report with her, away from the children playing outside on a beautiful sunny evening. Afterwards Sabah was extraordinarily quiet and calm – it was Allah's will, she repeated. But months later, she said, 'I didn't sleep that night, and for two days I sat in the park with the children so they would run about and not see my tears.'

All this time she had received only one letter from her husband, written on 14 April 2003 – unknown to him, the day after their baby was born. She received it in August 2003. Over the months she would phone the Red Cross frequently, only to be told, sorry, nothing for you. She would phone again, unable to accept it. And she was one of several Guantanamo families bitterly disappointed at the time with their experiences with the Red Cross. The next letter arrived only in February 2005. She was radiant for days. 'For each child he has written special advice so they know he thinks of them. And for me, so much thoughtfulness.' But it was obvious to her from his words that he had not then read her letters, or seen the children's drawings and messages. (Only the previous month, January 2005, was Jamil finally given 13 letters from his wife that the US authorities had been withholding for more than two years, and some written dialogue could begin between them.)

By then Sabah knew much more about her husband's situation, not only from the first group of British ex-prisoners who had come home, but from the US lawyer, Brent Mickum, who had managed to visit her husband in autumn 2004 after a long legal battle. And in January 2005, the last of the British prisoners, including Moazzam Begg, came home and spoke to her on the phone. None of what she heard was reassuring, mainly because it was all so completely illogical and contradictory. 'I think that human rights here have taken an open holiday', she said sadly, talking over what she had learned – none of it good.

The details kept her awake at night, when tears and despair came with the dark, though she could calm down by reading the Koran and repeating her firm conviction that Allah was looking after her and her husband. By day too she could never get the details out of her head, although she never let down her calm presence in front of the children.

She heard that Jamil was interrogated only five times in Guantanamo, unlike other men who had hundreds of interrogations, and that he was once told by his US interrogator, 'We're trying to get you out of here – we know you're an innocent man.' Nevertheless, a writ of *habeas corpus* failed, she learned – another layer of hope chipped away. The Guantanamo Combatant Status Review Tribunal – a military court – found Jamil was 'properly classified as an enemy combatant and was part of or supporting al-Qaida forces'.

Unclassified documents from the tribunal gave her a taste of the Alice-in-Wonderland style of the proceedings. For one thing, the tribunal had his name wrong – they were using his father's name, Abdul Latif, rather than his own, Jamil. Then his friendship with the cleric Abu Qatada, described as 'an al-Qaida operative', was listed as the first point in the evidence against him. Jamil told the tribunal that he was 'one of hundreds' who used to pray with Abu Qatada. 'If I were any danger, then Great Britain would have put me in prison.' Sabah was frightened by the absolute lack of logic in Guantanamo.

Another charge stated: 'The detainee was arrested in Gambia while attempting to board an airplane with equipment that resembled a homemade electronic device.' Sabah knew what had been in the public domain for two years: that the first, brief, arrest had taken place in the UK; that the battery charger was not in his luggage but in that of his Iraqi friend Bisher al Rawi – also in Guantanamo – and anyway, there was nothing suspicious about it, it was a battery charger bought from an Argos catalogue. How could the Americans *not* know all this, she asked? There was no answer.

Her mind could not take in the picture of her husband when she heard that Jamil had told the tribunal that in Gambia, Americans wearing black hoods kidnapped him, handcuffed him, cut off his clothes and flew him to Bagram, where he was kept underground without sight of light for two weeks. 'I was surprised that the Americans would do such a thing, it shocked me.'

By then Sabah knew enough to realise that false accusations under torture, or as a plea bargain, were routine in the system that had developed in the US prisons of the war on terror and which had taken her husband from her. She went over and over in her mind how it could have happened, who it might have been that named Jamil to the Americans. But there were no easy answers during her sleepless nights. Britain was her home, where she had come to be safe, how could she accept that some powerful part of Britain was responsible for the disaster that had overtaken her family.

One of the Tipton young men, Asif Iqbal, told Sabah that Jamil confided that the Americans had told him he would be sent back to Jordan, which made him terrified at the thought that he would be tortured or killed. Sabah's resort as always was prayer. 'I pray all the time and I know my God is there. I pray for my husband's strength.'

One of her own supports failed in May 2005 with the death of Mark Jennings, a gentle caring man who had been an assistant to Ed Davey, the MP for Bisher's family, and had gone out of his way on a personal basis to try to help not only them but also Jamil's family too, with initiatives such as Anas's letter to the Prime Minister. Mark Jennings took his own life, burned out, he wrote in the letter he left behind, by the strain of knowing what Guantanamo meant and finding that despite all his hard work for the prisoners and their families he could not affect anything. That same month Sabah gave me a bi-lingual Koran. I thought it was her way of saying, don't be like Mark, but she was too subtle to make any such point overtly.

Her own strength behind her reserved, private exterior grew. Her resilience and ingenuity had already enabled her to learn English well enough to cope with British bureaucracy, the routine problems of housing, transport, schools, hospitals, the illnesses and upsets of five children, a birth without her husband, the horror of his interminable incarceration and her sense of being in a limbo in which the Red Cross was her only faint lifeline to him.

She liked to dwell on the unexpected anonymous kindnesses she had had in Britain, out of the blue, such as food left at the door after she had her baby, an electric car race track given to the boys by prisoners who had returned, as well as offers of money, which she always said she did not need. These things gave her great pleasure and she always said it was the work of Allah. But at the same time she was deeply hurt by the loss of some Muslim former friends who, perhaps fearing the taint of 'terrorism', abandoned her. 'Can you imagine these people even blocked my telephone calls? But my God sent me other friends, and very kind people to help me, like our solicitor Gareth Peirce.'

Sometimes other veiled women sat round her kitchen table, chatting while their children played in the garden or watched TV. Usually they too were women with husbands imprisoned – in the UK in Belmarsh or Broadmoor, with secret charges of terrorism links. They too were managing to thrive on small moments of pleasure together when they would all forget for an hour or so the complete uncertainty of their futures. They came especially when Sabah's mother came once on a visit from Jordan. Her mother, as calm and smiling as Sabah, planted a little row of salad and broad beans in the garden – the habits of home brought to London.

Once I told Sabah that I had a Palestinian visitor who ran a clinic for disabled children in the Palestinian camps in Beirut, and was herself disabled, but very resourceful at managing. Sabah appeared at the door the following day to welcome her to London and shower her with presents to take back to the Palestinian children in Lebanon's camps.

In those years I learned to stop making mistakes such as buying new Eid clothes for the children from Marks and Spencer (which many Palestinians boycott) and having to take them back, or buying Haribo sweets and having them quietly given back by a nine year old who knew they contained gelatin, which is not *halal*. During the Eid holidays Sabah's row of little boys dressed in white clothes and caps sat on the sofa in the evenings with fingers tracing verses from the Koran, which they spoke aloud. Sabah photographed the children in their Eid best, to send to Guantanamo, never knowing when or if her husband would see the pictures, but always saying she knew that he would.

Once, at an after-school party event in their primary school, the children did a show and played games, while in the background a loop of film played over several times the iconic death of the 12-year-old Palestinian Mohamed Dura, sheltered unsuccessfully from Israeli fire by his father against a concrete pillar in Gaza during the second intifada. Already these transported children of Palestinians had a different universe in their heads than their surroundings in London.

Their own different identity became a problem for them when there were incidents with other children in school taunting them sometimes about their father, saying he was a terrorist locked up in Guantanamo. Even the smallest would call Sabah to 'see Daddy' when a picture of the orange jumpsuits of Guantanamo appeared on the television. 'Don't worry, that is not your Daddy,' Sabah used to say. She had for years been vague to them about why he was 'late coming home', and there were stories of problems with his passport. But then, as they got bigger and saw Guantanamo often on the television, she asked me to sit with the bigger boys and explain a bit of what had happened to their father and where was Cuba. Sabah herself could not explain to them what was inexplicable to her. The most important thing seemed to be to reassure them that their Dad didn't do anything wrong, it was a terrible mistake made by other men in America, and he would be home soon. But the little faces did not look convinced. And the time came later when the children did not want anyone to even speak about Guantanamo. 'They want the whole story to go away. They won't let any boys at school mention their Dad.'

After months and years of no progress on Jamil's case or the other UK residents, although the UK citizens had all been returned from Guantanamo, Sabah took the brave and surprising step for a woman with her background to begin to campaign publicly for her husband. She learned how to use the underground, to go to lawyers' offices, to the House of Commons, to meetings, to 10 Downing Street. She enlisted her MP, the Liberal Democrat Sarah Teather, she spoke to her local paper. She wrote open letters and statements, for public meetings about Guantanamo, at Amnesty or locally in her children's school, and had me read them for her. Her son Anas also began to read his own letters to his Dad at Amnesty meetings and to do some TV interviews. But Sabah worried about him: 'He's a child, and he should not know so much. Also, he above all of them needs his father here.' It was very hard for her to see her son go through disappointment and anger when, despite his great efforts, nothing changed for his father.

In October 2006 she had the first big breakthrough, thanks to her lawyers' persistence and the Red Cross. Sabah was able to speak to Jamil for an hour on the telephone, from inside the American embassy – a daunting place for her to enter. Jamil's mother had died earlier in the year and she had been devastated for weeks at the thought of the effect this would have on him. After the conversation with her husband she told me, 'There are no words for the emotion when I heard his voice … afterwards I went home to the children and I told them, Dad is fine, don't worry, he'll come soon, he kisses you all, he knows you are good children.' A few days later, during Eid prayers in the mosque, she was hugged and congratulated by many women she didn't even know, but who had heard about the phone call from Guantanamo. Sabah was her modest, gracious self in public, but at home later she said sadly, 'But no one knows except Allah what is happening for me, what is in my heart.'

Sometimes she would talk about how long the nights alone were, and how sometimes her dreams of her husband were too vivid. Once, she said sadly, in a dream he came home – 'But I must tell you he did not smile.'

In these years, with the stalemate in US legal proceedings, and the loss of hope there, lawyers were at work in parallel court cases in London to force the UK government to bring back the British residents as they had the UK citizens. She tried to understand and follow every detail. Once, in the High Court for a hearing for Jamil, Bisher and another prisoner from Britain, a Libyan named Omar Deghayes, Sabah, in her long black coat and small white headscarf, dared herself to approach the head of the Home Office legal team before the court started, and she just asked him if he had any children. They spoke for a few minutes and then she sat down at the back of the small court room, sure that he was 'a nice man' and would not pursue the objections to Jamil's return. But she had no experience of British establishment hypocrisy.

The case went inexorably on, and then she had to face the shock of hearing that for Bisher, her husband's great friend, the case against his return was being dropped by the UK government. She thought of Jamil being alone in Guantanamo, without his clever, English-speaking friend to rely on. Bisher, a kind, affable public school boy brought up in Britain, had years before been a very useful go-between and translator for British Intelligence with some of the Arab men, like Abu Qatada, who they wanted to arrest in the aftermath of 9/11. Despite that history of him working with them, the authorities had facilitated the arrest in Gambia, and then left Bisher in prisons in Afghanistan and Guantanamo all those years. Nothing showed Sabah more clearly how, for the state, men like her husband were expendable. But still she maintained to the children that anger was wrong, prayer for strength and patience was the answer.

At the same time, other US lawyers tried desperate unorthodox routes to free Jamil. One went to Jordan and met with high officials in the security services who gave him assurances that if Jamil came back to Jordan, nothing bad would happen to him. Sabah listened carefully to the American lawyer explaining this, not knowing whether to trust her instinct to refuse or, in the urgency of the desire to cut through the stalemate, to try this new idea. There was no one for her or her lawyers to refer to who had access to power in the US, in the UK, in Jordan, and who could advise her with confidence. There was yet another layer of total confusion for her when she heard that the Spanish government had announced they had a case against Jamil.

In Guantanamo Jamil went through similar reasoning when Spanish interrogators came to talk to him, and he was told that the Spanish government wanted to question him about his links to someone linked to Al Qaeda. The story made no sense to him, but he wondered, should he accept to go to Spain and face court there, just in order to get out of Guantanamo? In the end he, and another prisoner from Britain, the Libyan, Omar Deghayes, did sign the paper accepting to go to Spain. Jamil's Washington lawyer met repeatedly with the Spanish embassy asking for a trial to be set in Spain, and relayed this to Sabah. But the Spanish authorities then forgot about them in Guantanamo for several years and nothing happened. None of the small details she heard of this was comprehensible to Sabah. She would dream of the day when it would all be over, she said, and she could live somewhere quiet with her family, and try to forget and make herself forgive.

In the spring of 2007 Bisher was brought back to Britain. He visited Sabah's children immediately. The emotion for him seeing them, and speaking to Sabah, with her young son present in the room as the male of their family, was overwhelming for them all. It was August that year when the British government finally asked for Jamil and Omar to be brought back. For Sabah it was a big change of government attitude from the shameful refusal of responsibility for them during the Blair years, but one which was hard to trust. Home Secretaries and Foreign Office Ministers came and went, but all had stoutly maintained, including in successive court cases where the government side was argued by top British lawyers, that these men's fate was not Britain's problem.

And it was December 2007 before the two men flew in.

That night Sabah and the children were ready for him, in new clothes, with the house decorated and special food on the table. But late in the evening she got a phone call from the airport, from her lawyer Gareth Peirce, to say that there was a problem and her husband would not, after all, be home that night. She was devastated, despite reassurance that it was not serious. Her instinct was right – it was very serious.

On the plane, unknown to their lawyers, Spanish extradition papers were served on the two men. They would have to appear for an extradition hearing at Westminster magistrates' court at 10 a.m. the following morning. During the night sureties had to be found to try to get bail for them, and one who came forward was Vanessa Redgrave. In the morning Sabah was outside the court room – Jamil had sent a message through the lawyers that he did not want her to see him first in court, after all this time. Peeping through the crack in the door she saw her husband, shockingly transformed with a waist length white beard.

The last-minute decision to subject the two men to extradition warrants from Spain on unsubstantiated allegations of terrorism, which meant they had to appear in court immediately to contest deportation, marked yet another low point in the British government's handling of these cases. For Sabah, and for Omar's brother, it felt like torture, they said, waiting, knowing nothing, outside that courtroom.

Sabah could only pray quietly in the crowded corridor, as she could not hear what went on inside. Edward Fitzgerald QC castigated Spain's role in the ordeal of their last five years:

> They acquiesced to, and facilitated, their interrogation at Guantanamo and indeed participated in that interrogation process. They took no steps or adequate steps to say 'we want them for trial in Spain'. They left them to be interrogated in Guantanamo, and now – after they have been exonerated by US authorities, after English police have said they don't wish to bring any charges – the Spanish authorities are saying, 'we want to question them on the self same charges'.[1]

Fitzgerald and a second QC, Tim Otty, had little trouble in politely batting off the government's extremely weak case for opposing bail for Jamil, the first case heard. The Spanish allegations were so vague and old – dating back to 2003 – it was astonishing, the lawyers said, that the government could take them seriously and go so far as actually to oppose bail to a man who had survived five years of Guantanamo – put there by the British government – and was about to be reunited with his family.

The tension broke for Sabah when she heard the two men had got bail, with curfews and electronic tags, until the New Year. She and Jamil were helped through a media crush and into a taxi home to the children, one of whom Jamil had never seen.

But the electronic tag and the 7 p.m. curfew for Jamil were scary daily reminders to Sabah for several months that the ordeal was not over. Even with him before her eyes, she knew she was still in danger of losing her husband again. The parties and celebrations the children wanted so badly would have to wait. It was several months before the case collapsed when the Spanish magistrate refused permission to Judge Balthazar Garzon to bring the case. Spain did not want a public airing of the involvement of Spanish intelligence agents in interrogations of the men in Guantanamo Bay and overflights of Spain in rendition cases. Guantanamo was by then becoming an embarrassment in Europe and was meant to be forgotten, like its victims. When Sabah finally heard the case was over, the tag would come off, the curfew was finished, she found it so hard to believe that she had to phone her solicitor repeatedly to confirm it, as 7.00 p.m. drew near and Jamil was piling the children in the car to go out to celebrate like any other family.

*   *   *

On 30 June 2010 in a ceremony in the Sir Richard Eyre Theatre at the College of North West London, decked with lights and stars and little tables for soft drinks, Sabah was presented with a small statuette and a certificate of 'Outstanding Achievement' in the Faculty of Skills for Life. Her extraordinary determination had seen her choose to wear the *hijab* as a teenager against her family's advice, had taken her far away from her family to Pakistan with her new husband, then had made her at home with her children in Britain, a country where she did not know the language well, and where she fought a lonely five-year battle against the power of the state for her husband's release, and willed Jamil to keep strong through his ordeal in Guantanamo. That determination had kept her going through two years of a British college course, despite poor health, and waves of utter accumulated fatigue. For her, it was all through Allah's gifts for her, and she said, smiling, that she considered herself a happy woman.

2
Zinnira: From Medina to Guantanamo

'He's still my Valentine.'

In Zinnira's parents's flat she sat very quietly on the sofa, wanting to hold hands and talking so softly it was difficult to hear her. The words were so sad that they were difficult to listen to. She talked about her dreams and the bad thoughts and bad voices in her head. The voices told her sometimes that her husband had divorced her while he was in Guantanamo, or they told her he was dead. And the voices came and went and came again insistently with those messages that were her deepest fears. Then she became obsessed by the wish to go immediately to paradise and forget this world.

In the darkest days when all her efforts to block the voices out failed, she was deeply depressed and unreachable. Medication made her sleepy and days slipped away in sleep and half sleep. Some days she asked softly for reassurance that the voices' words were untrue, and sometimes the reassurance worked, at least for a moment, and her shy smile flashed. Her mother sat across the room, a small warm presence in a white sari quietly reading the Koran. Sometimes Zinnira had to be in hospital, but home with her parents was more comforting, although very stressful for an elderly couple who were both in poor health.

There was another Zinnira, who learned to drive, ran her own small house, took her four children to school, cooked and cleaned, taught extra classes after school and spent devoted hours in hospital sitting beside her mother after she had a serious operation. In the good times Zinnira took Arabic classes on the Internet so that when her Saudi husband returned from Guantanamo, he would be proud and happy with her. She made plans to learn sewing with her sister-in-law, and often looked after other children in the family as well as her four. She sent her husband letters and photos of the children through the Red Cross.

Zinnira's father had come from India, invited to be the Imam at a South London mosque after he had once been the guest preacher in Ramadan. And Zinnira was brought up in London – the baby in a family of eleven children. Going on the Hajj to Mecca with her father when she was 21 was her young girl's romantic dream come true. When she did go, she prayed that Allah would let her marry a man in white robes and a scarf, like those she saw during that intense experience. She never doubted that her prayer would be answered.

Back home in London, her prayer was answered, when a young man from Medina came to her father's mosque, and spoke to her mother about wanting to get married. Shaker Aamer visited the family flat, talked to Zinnira's parents and brothers about his plans to stay in Britain and his current work as an interpreter for lawyers. He was an attractive, confident, outgoing man, and everyone liked him. Zinnira liked him immediately, but was rather overwhelmed by him. He was very different from anyone she knew in her own community circle and, as she remembered later, he seemed at first, 'well, just too big really'.

But Shaker's kindness to her made her love him, and they were soon married. They were opposites in many ways, he was worldly, educated in the US as well as Saudi Arabia, she was a very sheltered South London girl with India as her hinterland; in contrast to her shyness, he was outgoing, talkative, always making friends with everyone. She laughed once as she told the story of how at their wedding he was chatting to the registrar so busily that she thought they must be friends from before. 'He's big, and strong, and talking, always talking to everyone, making friends with everyone – people always love him.'[1]

The couple had three small children when Shaker, like others in this book, and several of his friends, began to think about moving to Afghanistan to be part of what they believed would be building a pure Islamic state, and leaving Britain and Western culture behind for ever. In the aftermath of the defeat and retreat of the Soviet army, and then the apparent ousting of the various warlords by the Taliban, they saw Afghanistan as a chance to make Islamic dreams come true. Shaker discussed his plan with his father-in-law, who advised him to go ahead of his family first and see what he could organise. There were no anxieties – the war was over – but only practical questions to solve. (His father-in-law in his time had also made a life-changing move for his large family, in uprooting from India to Britain.)

Zinnira soon went too with the children. She adored her husband, would never have doubted his judgement for a moment, and settled down in Kabul looking after her babies, in a house shared with another young couple they knew from Birmingham, Moazzam Begg, Zeynab his wife and their children. While her husband plunged energetically into a new life of school construction and well digging, Zinnira felt very far away from her family and with conditions of daily life remote from her experience. But she felt her husband looked after her very carefully, and bought her a washing machine, which pleased her very much, and they were happy together and with their two boys and a girl.

Looking back years later, her friend Zeynab remembered how lovely their house had been, 'my husband found the best house, a big, big, house and I was downstairs and she was upstairs. She was very, very happy there, and Shaker was so pleased that she did come with the family – he made a big effort to make it nice for her, always having guests, he was such a generous person.' That life, and their happiness, ended after 9/11 and the subsequent US bombing of Afghanistan.

Years later, Zinnira's darknesses would usually come down towards the end of the year. She remembered the trauma of late 2001 and the departure from Afghanistan. She blamed herself for Shaker ending up in Guantanamo, because she had written to him saying that she was alright in Pakistan, where he had sent her and the children for safety, and he shouldn't worry about her, or rush back from Kabul where he was looking after their house. She was not alright in fact, she was terrified for him, frightened of how her life with the children had suddenly slipped into wholly unfamiliar territory which she could not negotiate without Shaker. But she wrote to him wanting to be reassuring, to be a good wife. The letter stuck painfully in her mind, perhaps if she had asked him to come at once, nothing would have happened to him, she believed.

This preoccupation with being a good wife was still at the centre of Zinnira's life for ten years after her husband's disappearance in Afghanistan. After eight years she marked off the sad milestone of when she had been away from him longer than she was with him. Sometimes people suggested she should divorce him, as other women in similar positions of limbo did, in this book, sometimes at their husband's initiative.

But life without Shaker was unthinkable for Zinnira. Shaker, even completely absent, was her life, her preoccupation as much in her times of sickness as in her optimistic times preparing herself and her children for a future life with him back in charge. Would they live in London or in Saudi Arabia? Everything would be Shaker's choice.

Far away and unbeknown to her in late 2001, Shaker had been captured by bounty hunters. Whoever they were, they thus earned the $5,000 for every Arab or other foreigner, which was promised in hundreds of thousands of US leaflets scattered in Pakistan and Afghanistan. They bartered him with two of the other armed groups that roamed the country in the chaos after the US bombing and entry with Special Forces troops after 9/11.

Shaker was finally handed over to the Americans and ended up in Guantanamo, after initial rough days of humiliation, interrogation and torture in Kandahar and Bagram, like Sabah's husband. However, it was a long time before Zinnira knew any of this, and the initial trauma of separation from him, when she was pregnant and especially vulnerable, scarred her very deeply. Her father, like Shaker's family in Saudi Arabia, believed his son-in-law had died in Afghanistan, until he chanced on a small paragraph naming Shaker as one of the men flown to Guantanamo Bay, and phoned the news to his son-in-law's Saudi family.

The birth of Zinnira's third son, Faris, in February 2002, without her husband at her side, was the real beginning of her hard London years as a single mother with the responsibility for four children, including one who had never seen his father. Even for the older ones, the years passed with Dad becoming more and more a remote abstraction. Their everyday childhood reality of school and home was dominated periodically by coping with their mother's times of deep sadness, sinking into mental illness, and the need to move in with their grandparents or one of their uncles until it passed. It was extremely difficult for them, and the boys had many of the same bruising experiences with their peers as Sabah's sons had.

Zinnira herself had to cope, like Sabah, with the sadness and fear of hearing of the British men coming home from Guantanamo in 2003 and 2004, but without her husband. Then she gradually had to learn something about the horrors these other men had endured, and feel her mind slip painfully into seeing her husband in that context. Hunger strikes, restraint chairs, shackling, solitary confinement, freezing cold cells, interrogations by women, sexual humiliations, were beyond anything she could bear to take in. She did not read newspapers, or watch television news, but sometimes well-meaning people brought her newspaper-cuttings, not realising how devastating they were to her. Her friends and her lawyers tried to shield her as much as possible from knowing the painful details.

Her husband's best friend, and the person who had shared the Kabul months with them, Moazzam Begg, came back from Guantanamo and visited them. That was a moment for a rare outburst of tears from the older children who, seeing him, suddenly remembered the different times with their Dad at home, times which Moazzam had been part of. Then over more years, after a great deal of litigation by their lawyers, another milestone passed when all the UK residents finally came home – except Shaker.

Meanwhile, in yet another milestone, Zinnira received a devastating letter from her husband:

> I am dying here every day, mentally and physically. This is happening to all of us. We have been ignored, locked up in the middle of the ocean for years. Rather than humiliate myself, having to beg for water, I would rather hurry up the process that is going to happen anyway. I would like to die quietly, by myself. I was once 250 pounds. I dropped to 150 pounds in the first hunger strike. I want to make it easy on everyone. I want no feeding, no forced tubes, no 'help', no 'intensive assisted feeding'. This is my legal right. The British government refuses to help me. What is the point of my wife being British? I thought Britain stood for justice, but they abandoned us, people who have lived in Britain for years, and who have British wives and children. I hold the British government responsible for my death, as I do the Americans.[2]

She could not believe her husband wrote like this of wanting to die, it was so out of character with the man she knew. She had had so few letters from him over the years, it was hard to hold on to the man she once knew. Over and over she asked everyone, why was it only him who had not come back? Why did no one know? Why did no one help him?

Over the years many people tried to help him, lawyers in Britain, lawyers in the US, lawyers with permission to visit Guantanamo. There were attempts by distinguished UK delegations to meet US officials at the highest levels, private meetings at the Foreign Office, public meetings in the community and in the House of Commons, where Zinnira's father spoke. There were marches and demonstrations of people dressed in orange suits and shackled. There were filmed appeals from the children on YouTube. There were women's deputations to Downing Street of politicians, actors, lawyers, which Zinnira's daughter joined, proud to be treated as an adult but, like Sabah's son, disillusioned after a while when nothing happened as a result of the initiatives adults pressed her to make.

Then sometimes word would come from Guantanamo Bay that Shaker did not want any campaigning, certainly not by his family in public, and then the photos of the children would be taken off websites in deference to his wishes. But his name was well enough known for the media still sometimes to pressure Zinnira, or her family, for interviews with her or the children. They never wanted to speak to journalists, and it brought tension in the family about whether they should – given that nothing else was working.

In 2007 Shaker was at last cleared for release, and a roller coaster of emotions swept the family. Miscommunication and confusion in the information from Guantanamo, the information coming from various lawyers, the information coming from the Foreign Office, made life more tense than ever. The family were told he would be allowed to go to Saudi Arabia, not the UK, then that he would be sent to another country, then that he had refused everything except a return to the UK.

At one point the children believed he was after all being sent back to Saudi Arabia and packed their little suitcases to go too. Once Zinnira got a phone call from Saudi Arabia from a recently released Saudi prisoner, saying that Shaker had been on the plane to leave with him, but was then taken off. It was a very hard time – hugely disorientating and stressful for her and for the children, and Zinnira's depressions, psychotic moments and retreats to her mother's house came and went.

Sometimes Zinnira found social workers or psychiatric nurses who visited her were consistent, helpful supports. But at other times she felt as though she had fallen off the official radar, and it was not clear who was really responsible for monitoring her fragile health. There was even a time when she got a letter discharging her as no longer needing visits, although she was still having fantasies and paranoia. And the medication seemed to cause her other problems such as memory loss, loss of concentration, feeling drowsy, even when she was relatively well and able to be at home. In an extraordinary failure of the social services system, no professional supported the children through the long ordeal as they needed to be supported. Many efforts were made by volunteers to find mentors for them, or to take them out to local children's activities, but as the years went by it became almost impossible to sustain the momentum.

After years of waiting in limbo for rare letters, Zinnira and the children, with her father, were finally able to talk to her husband on a Skype call organised through the Red Cross. She was happy beyond words. The children were shy with their Dad at first, but then extremely happy too, and believed it meant he would soon be home. But the calls were very rare, and sometimes he spoke instead to his family in Saudi. There was nothing certain for the family in London to hold onto. No one knew why he was not released, no one knew how to reach into the powers that held him, was it the US Secretary for Defense, was it the Secretary of State, was it Congressional leaders, was it the President of the United States?

Ten years after Shaker arrived in Guantanamo it was his youngest child's tenth birthday and Valentine's Day 2012. In a superhuman effort to keep her mind focused away from Guantanamo and images of her husband alone in his cell, Zinnira wrote the first poem she had written for years, a touching, hopeful love poem. Months later she was back in her mother's care, persecuted by the voices and painful fantasies.

A Heart of Gold
For my beloved Shaker Aamer
In 10 years of waiting

You cared for me and were ever,
On my side when I needed a favour,
I cannot forget you, no ... never ...
Time is new and your memories old
Cause you have a heart of gold

You made my dreams come true,
In my hardship helped me through,
Without you, what I would do?
Your insistence cannot be sold,
Cause you have a heart of gold.

You are the roof over my head,
You are the shadow that can't be lead,
You are my voice when the silence breaks,
Your hand I seek, your hand I hold,
Cause you have a heart of gold.

You show me light in the dark,
And you guide me when I am lost,
Your happiness is all I ask,
But your story remains untold,
Cause you have a heart of gold.

Your smile is like a new pearl,
Come, I will hide you like a treasure,
Though now the life is sad and dull,
In my heart of sorrow I feel warm,
Cause you have a heart of gold.

In my face is your reflection,
In my mind is your remembrance,
In my heart is your affection,
And the whole world can behold.

3

Dina and Josephine: From Palestine and Africa to House Arrest in London

'My husband, he tried to hurt himself ... several times, well, to end his life.'

When a burly, smiling man with terrible English called Mahmood arrived at my front door unannounced one day in 2005, looking for Moazzam Begg, I was new enough to the world he lived in to be surprised. I was surprised that he knew who I was, where I lived and that Moazzam would probably be there as we were working on his book. I had heard Mahmood's name as one of the Belmarsh men, now on a Control Order, and one who was unusually vociferous in public about the damage that regime had done to him, but I knew no more details than that. And I also didn't know then that a person on a Control Order was not allowed by the Home Office to make appointments to meet people, but could only meet them by chance – hence his abrupt arrival at my house. Nor did I know then about Mahmoud's extraordinarily obsessive personal information system on everyone connected, however tangentially, to his own drama, and his detailed knowledge, constantly updated on the phone, of everything happening in his homeland – Gaza – and instantly spread. This was the identity he had created for himself in this period of his life – the man who knew everything. It was a fragile replacement for the can-do, resourceful, driven man of an earlier life.

That afternoon I watched the two young men on the sofa drinking tea, chatting, looking through a file of photographs of children, of wells dug and schools built in Afghanistan, which Mahmood had brought with him. I saw the huge insistence and pride when Mahmood showed the well that was named after Moazzam's oldest son. There was an unsettling intensity about Mahmood, but it seemingly dissipated in the happy, comradely conversation of shared experience between these two very different men who had not seen each other during the years when Moazzam had been in Guantanamo and Mahmood in Belmarsh and Broadmoor. The ease of their afternoon together didn't strike me as unusual then. But I often remembered it in later years, when the darkness really started to come down over Mahmood and his family, and I would too often hear one side of a long, patient conversation on the phone as Moazzam tried to calm him, or I saw him angry at home, or even angrier when he was in hospital on hunger strike. I remembered it even more sharply later, when things became worse and the Home Office, in an act of cruel stupidity, decreed that Mahmood could no longer contact Moazzam – an emotional lifeline.

The Control Order men were all refugees from countries such as Algeria, Jordan, Palestine, Libya or Tunisia, to which they could not be sent back, as it was accepted then that they would risk arrest, torture or even death there. They were arrested in the UK in December 2001, as part of the post-9/11 worldwide intelligence swoop on Muslims. They were assessed as 'risks to national security' and sent to Belmarsh high security prison in London. They mostly did not know each other, were mainly products of very different cultures and educational and political experiences, and were all utterly bewildered to find themselves arrested together. When they were each told that they were suspected of links to Al Qaeda, most of them had never heard of Al Qaeda until 11 September 2001.[1] They then found that they were being held on secret evidence that was not disclosed to their lawyers and about which they were never interrogated nor charged. Several of them were personally familiar with such imprisonments in their own home countries, but all of them had come to Britain precisely because they thought such things could not happen here. They had all relished a feeling of personal security for the first time in years. A sense of stunned incomprehension gradually soured to a deep sense of betrayal. The prison revived previous prison trauma for some, depression set in for many and the secret evidence left them with a feeling of hopelessness against a powerful system they could not engage. Indefinite detention felt like torture to them and as life suspended for their frightened wives.

After just over two long years in Belmarsh prison, some of the group, in desperation, wrote a letter to the *Guardian*:

> We were arrested in December 2001 and taken straight to Belmarsh prison. We know that the police in this country have enormous powers to investigate suspected terrorists. Why did no one ever speak to us? Why were we never asked a single question before being locked up as terrorists? We have never had a trial. We were found guilty without one. We are imprisoned indefinitely and probably forever. We have no idea why. We have not been told what the evidence is against us. We are here. Speak to us. Listen to us. Tell us what you think and why. If you did, you would no longer believe we were a threat to this country. You would think perhaps that there was not the emergency you have imagined here. Everyone is giving their opinion about us. Why not think of coming to us first, rather than locking us up and never speaking to us?

They signed it, 'The forgotten detainees'.[2]

They had indeed more or less disappeared from the national consciousness. And, had anyone – besides their lawyers – thought about them, it would not have been with any sympathetic questions about their legal rights. The label of terrorist was indelibly on them, and in the general mood of fear of what might lie behind the war on terror, which was being stoked by government and media, the anonymous men and their families were easily forgotten.

By then eight of the men were suffering from mental illness and four of those were in florid psychosis, which got them transferred to Broadmoor Secure Mental Hospital.[3] One of those was Mahmood, after the first of a number of suicide attempts. Three of the men, assessed for their lawyers by a team of psychiatrists, were found to have been already suffering mental health problems associated with their torture or prison experience at home, when they were first sent to Belmarsh. The psychiatrists reported to the Royal College of Psychiatrists that the eight detainees who were seen by eleven psychiatrists and one psychologist were 'all clinically depressed and a number had PTSD ... and the indefinite nature of the detention was a major factor in their deterioration'. They suffered 'helplessness and hopelessness'.[4] The men were in a unique situation, the doctors said.

There was another side to many of these detainees though, only shown to the world some years later in an extraordinary art exhibition of their work produced in Belmarsh and Long Lartin prisons. One huge, intricate mosque was made of 25,000 matchsticks and took 1,000 hours of work over one year and four months. Others had made a jewellery box for a wife, others hundreds of paintings of the darkness of imprisonment or lyrical scenes of flowers or the sea, others elaborate pottery. Poetry poured from some men.

Nearly two more years passed before the House of Lords ruled, in December 2004, that these foreigners could not be imprisoned indefinitely in Britain, just as no British person could be. The following March they were released on strict bail conditions and a new kind of house arrest known as Control Orders was introduced for terrorism suspects who could not be deported, and they lived at home subject to very stringent conditions. The psychiatrists noted that the restrictions aggravated the men's depression and anxiety in some cases. One single severely disabled man was placed in a completely unadapted flat, others in areas where they knew no one and had no support. The men were made anonymous, to be known as Mr A or Mr VV, by court order from the Special Immigration Appeals Commission (SIAC), established in 1997 as the sole appeal court for foreign nationals whom the Home Secretary wished to deport on national security grounds, when some of the evidence against them was too secret to be disclosed. This dehumanising anonymity was refused by Mahmoud.

In 2001 SIAC's remit was extended and it became the appeal court for all the Belmarsh men over the next decade of legal contests against deportations, prison and the conditions of Control Orders. An Orwellian system was devised for SIAC, of special advocates, senior lawyers, all QCs, with security clearance, who could see the evidence against their clients but who could not have any contact either with the clients themselves or their main lawyers. Some soon rebelled against the SIAC system and resigned as special advocates, notably Ian Macdonald QC, who said that his role was 'to provide a false legitimacy to indefinite detention without knowledge of the accusations being made and without any kind of criminal charge or trial. For me this is untenable.' In the same year, one of the original three lay members of the Commission, former ambassador Sir Brian Barder, KCMG, resigned.[5] He said that the rulings of two higher courts, where the Home Secretary had appealed against a SIAC decision, taken as a whole appeared 'to establish as part of English law that the Home Secretary may deport an immigrant without having to show that any single one of his past activities contributes towards a case for deportation. He may act in this way merely on the grounds of his belief that future activities of the person concerned might threaten national security, however indirectly.' SIAC, he said, had become toothless, and the Home Secretary's powers 'virtually unaccountable'.[6]

Home Secretaries came and went through the years of Labour Party power and then a coalition government, and, despite manifold efforts by lawyers and others, none of them could ever be persuaded to take a close look at the Control Order families, to understand what the measures meant to the families that lived these constricted lives. New measures brought in by the coalition government were called Terrorism

Prevention and Investigation Measures (TPims), but they did not alter anything substantive.

When Mahmood was arrested with the others in 2001 and an outpouring of media reports on 'terrorists' followed, his wife, Dina, also a Palestinian, though from Hebron in the West Bank, kept it secret. She told almost no one in Britain and not even her family back in Jordan. She moved to a different part of London with her five children and put them in a different school. Another young woman in the same situation so feared the whole family being stigmatised as linked to a terrorist, and worrying that her baby daughter would not be treated in her local surgery, that she presented herself as a single mother. Another, Josephine, the French/Senegalese wife of one of the Algerians, did not manage to see her husband in Belmarsh for six months, and was absolutely without support until lawyers found her husband and then came to see her and organise a visit to him. All these women managed their new, frightening and lonely lives with extraordinary resilience – usually much better than their husbands – through the four years of prison, maintaining that it was all a ghastly mistake and their husbands would soon be released.

Prison visits, after long bus journeys, followed by routine searches and sniffer dogs, and initially no physical contact with him, were the younger children's formative experience of their fathers. One described the first sight of her father, then on hunger strike.

> He was very skinny, he looked very ill. I felt very sorry for him but we were only allowed to talk to him with a glass between us and talking using a phone between us and there was an interpreter in the visit. Then, after a few visits we were allowed to visit our Dad but in a place where it had lots of people but it was very uncomfortable.

And, from another child, 'When we went to visit him in prison it took us about two hours to get there and dogs used to smell us and I used to hate dogs.'

Eight years later all Mahmood's children remembered every detail of the traumatic day of their father's arrest.[7]

It was the second day of Eid … it was the worst Eid I ever had … early in the morning and we were sleeping … it was so scary … bang, bang, bang and there were lots of police in our bedroom … my mum was crying, our baby was crying … downstairs the police were sitting in our room smoking … they took my dad away, and we had to go to a hotel while they searched our house … when they took us home at night time everything was messy and untidy.

Their mother too remembered every detail of the day which started eight years of a very traumatic life: the police guns, the swearing at her husband and throwing him to the ground to be handcuffed, the children so frightened that some wet themselves, being taken away from their home. Days later press photographs showed their house, with a headline about a 'terrorist raid', then rubbish was thrown at the door, neighbours spat at her, her face veil was pulled off three times. For 40 days she kept phoning the police to try to find out where her husband was. Then came the first prison visit, when she found Mahmood on hunger strike and weak in a wheelchair, and subsequent ones when he was only allowed to speak Arabic in one of every four visits, although his English was far from fluent.

Mahmood could not tolerate Belmarsh – it brought too many echoes of the Israeli prison experience that had marked his early life – and he was often crying when he phoned home. He was among those transferred to Broadmoor Secure Mental Hospital. For Dina this was another heavy blow and years later she marked it as the beginning of her husband's acute vulnerability.

I could not visit him whilst he was there, I tried, but whenever I went there I was told he was in isolation, in solitary confinement. Broadmoor prison was very far from our home, it was very difficult travelling with 5 children only to be sent back home, to be told your husband is in isolation. It was around this time that my husband began to self-harm. He drank detergents, he used pens to dig deep into his arms.

As Mahmoud's ability to tolerate the absolute uncertainty of his situation grew less, Dina's dignity was unshakeable and she was the children's rock. They kept up at school, homework was done, their bedrooms were neat.

Josephine's Algerian husband was the first of the men to get bail, six months before the House of Lords ruling, on compassionate grounds as he had become seriously depressed, and so weak he was dependent on a wheelchair instead of the crutches he had used previously as a polio victim. 'He was starting to be too much depressed ... too depressed. Prison was killing him slowly', Josephine said. Releasing him on bail, Judge Collins said he wanted them to have a normal family life with their little girl. But the judge could not have imagined what a long way it was going to be from normal, and how rapidly it would sour after the first few months. For nine months Mr G's house arrest was total.

> He couldn't go out at all ... Doctor, hospital, nothing. No visitor at all. Even my daughter and me, no visitors. Even the solicitor, it took maybe three months to be cleared to come and visit him. And he was not allowed any phone, even the home phone, he was not allowed ... Mr G, why did they even take his name away?

Mr G had an electronic tag, which monitored him, and he could never go out of the house, but even so, he had to phone the tagging company on a special phone five times a day to say he was still in the house. 'It was every four hours. The last one was in the middle of the night. It is nonsense. This drive him mad.' He would not be the only one to be driven mad by a Control Order phone. Mahmood, once home, would frequently lose his temper with the machine when it failed to pick up his number. The phones often malfunctioned too, and men would be arrested and taken back to SIAC for a hearing. Sometimes, if they were lucky and had a witness who was not a family member, they were freed, but sometimes they went back to prison for an apparent breach of the Control Order, which they denied. On their network, everyone knew when it happened and a chill of fear ran round.

When the fathers came home on the Control Orders, the children were thrilled, but soon disappointment hit them as they found life transformed by the restrictions that were on them too – no Internet for homework, no mobile phones for calling friends and a father very different from how they remembered him.

However, after the spring of 2005, prison was not yet over for Mr G and the others released from Belmarsh and Broadmoor on Control Orders with their tags, phone obligations, curfews, restricted geographic boundaries and isolation from friends and acquaintances. After the terrorist attacks in London on 7 July 2005, they were all re-arrested in August and taken to Long Lartin prison in Worcestershire. Two months later Mr G tried to commit suicide by hanging himself from his wheelchair.

Josephine went to court to see his lawyers try, and succeed, to get him bail again. His blue bruised neck and sick, shattered look were unanswerable testimony of his frailty, and he went home to new years of life ruled by the Control Order's limits and the nagging fear of incurring even a minor breach, which could mean a five-year prison sentence. 'It's very tough, always I'm worrying about his time. We know people who that happened to – they went back in Belmarsh', Josephine said. Her husband's geographic limit included the mosque, his daughter's school and the shops. He was allowed to leave the house for two hours in the middle of the day, but each time he left or returned he had to call the tagging company. The company had the right to visit him at home unannounced at any time. Invariably, she said with resignation, the company staff came at night, spent a long time, and in examining the special phone and its box they would disturb her daughter and later the two babies the couple had.

The conditions during this second time on bail were better, as Mr G could use the fixed telephone in the house and often spoke to his mother in Algeria. Also, he could go into a part of the small garden behind the flat during the hours when his curfew was relaxed, though he could not speak to any of the other users of the garden. In the early months of knowing Josephine I did not yet have official clearance to visit the flat, but she was quite happy to put on her coat and her *hijab* and chat from a chair in the doorway herself, with a chair outside the flat for her visitor and coffee and biscuits balanced on a stool.

She laughed telling the stories of the extraordinary hoops the family had to jump through to be sure not to break the bail conditions.

My first washing machine story was when I was pregnant, and we had to wait I don't know how many weeks for the man to be allowed to come and mend it when it was broken, and then my husband had to go into the other room so he didn't see him or speak to him. But my second washing machine story, how many years later, was even more crazy – they delivered the new machine early in the morning, and my husband had to tell them to leave it outside the flat, which they thought was weird as surely someone would take it away before the plumber came, and they saw he was in a wheelchair and they really wanted to help by bringing it inside. 'No, no, no, thank you, thank you', my husband was saying to them – he was not going to explain that he was not allowed to have anyone enter without Home Office ok

... In the end I had to push it in myself – and it was really, really, heavy, and I couldn't even just leave it inside the door, as then my husband's wheelchair could not pass. Then I was ringing the solicitor, and she needed the name of the plumber who was coming after the delivery men, to get permission from the Home Office for him to enter, but the plumbing company could not say the name of which man would come. It was stalemate. In the evening my solicitor hired a different plumber and told the Home Office his name, and he came, and the man from the Home Office came at the same time. Then after all that, the man from the Home Office just sat there on the sofa and never even went downstairs to see the plumber fixing the machine. So, we'd paid two plumbers. For what?

Rules and regulations from the Home Office governed every aspect of family life. There were court cases about timings of curfew hours, which were different in school time and in holiday time. 'And my husband gets confused, even I get confused, why don't they just keep the same time always?' After five years passed, and at another court hearing, her daughter, just in secondary school, was given permission to use the Internet for homework. For the family, it was a gift, a treat they had not expected.

Then came a new problem when her husband's second leg had to have a plastic splint fitted as his strength deteriorated, and it meant moving the electronic tag off his leg. A recent court case involving another Algerian man they knew had alarmed Josephine acutely.

Is my husband going to have it on his wrist, now? These tags scare me now after someone we know went back to prison because they said in court he had tried to take it off – can you imagine, him with little children at home who are his life, and a wife who depends on him, doing something so stupid ... for what?

The strange circumstances of her life left Josephine remarkably unfazed, and it would be hard to find a more optimistic, even-tempered person, who, miraculously, brought up her children with the same sunny temperament. She liked London, comparing it favourably with France and the open Islamophobia she felt there, and where she always felt the need to take off her *hijab* on the Eurostar when going to visit her family.

Josephine spoke to her mother every day, had her mother and a sister to stay for long periods – always having to get Home Office permission for the exact period. Her mother-in-law – with whom she did not share a common language – stayed for months. Visiting her, it was always easy to forget what a miracle she was doing in her life, in a one bedroom flat, by making all these people's lives remarkably happy.

But the shadow of how her husband had been changed, by the prison years and then by his constricted life, was always there.

> My husband before, he was very joyful, always laughing, just like my baby Ishmael now. It was very nice when we were first together, very happy. But when he came out of prison he became paranoid. He was always thinking everybody is watching him even here at home, and the time he goes outside he is always scared. He's doing nightmares, he's screaming at night, he was too much seeing people coming, he has medication and once they sent him to a mental hospital, but he couldn't stay there, he was locked up all the time. Now he don't speak much like before. He's closing himself off, even from me. It's difficult, it's difficult.

Over the years many efforts were made to find another country that would take the family to let them start a new life without restrictions. Requests were made by intermediaries to countries in Latin America, and to Africa, even thinking of a faint connection to coup-ridden Guinea Bissau, but it was not the political moment for governments to make such individual acts of solidarity, and the answer was always no, or just silence. And, as Josephine put it, 'once the British called us terrorists, who will believe us, instead of a powerful government?' As a result Mr G was one of the men with nightmares, one of those who would spend days, weeks, months or even years in mental hospitals, and one of many who became dependent on medication to function.

It was 2007 before I went to Mahmoud's house to meet his family, still knowing little about the texture of their lives. They lived in a little maisonette in West London, with a patio filled with drying clothes and children's bikes in front of the door. In the neat sitting room, three girls in their early teens took turns looking after the baby or helping their mother make the tea. They talked shyly at first, about how one of them wanted to be a writer and the other two dreamed of being doctors – ambitions that gave their highly educated mother evident pleasure to hear, perhaps a reminder of the life she could have expected for herself when she had finished university in Jordan. Her girls had an unworldly air to them, a product of Dina's fierce protection and carefully taught manners and the traditions of Palestinian hospitality. The spotless kitchen, with everything scrubbed and put away immediately after every meal, was like Sabah's, like so many Palestinian women's homes I had seen, in Gaza, in the West Bank, in the camps of Lebanon and Syria – order valued and maintained in the private sphere – the defence against the uncontrollable outside world.

This home was on the surface a scene of normality, a close, strict family life, where the children did well at school, and in addition Dina taught them herself because she found the British schools too full of outings and projects and not enough hard work. She supervised what they watched on television, looked over their homework, had them helping with cooking and cleaning, and shared everything with the older ones. They had few visitors, partly because of the constraints of the Control

Order and people's fear of the vetting system, plus alienation because of the stigma of terrorism around Control Orders.

After the group of men came out of Belmarsh in 2005, Mahmoud was in a different situation from the others because he was from Gaza and was stateless, so there was never any judicial contest, as with the Libyans, the Algerians and the Jordanians, to deport them home on an assurance from the state in question that they would not be tortured. Initially, besides his electronic tag and his curfew, he had to report daily to a police station. Within a week he had tried to commit suicide using a cocktail of his drugs and was in a coma in hospital for three days. Later his frustration with the regime of controls often exploded in a public drama in the police station. In one of the myriad court appeals of these years some of these conditions were dropped, and his curfew was only for the night – 7 p.m. to 7 a.m.

However, the house was still his prison, and it became a prison in many ways for the whole family. It was a prison where the police presence was only too frequent, with intrusive raids, including going through Dina's own clothes and the children's clothes and toys. Many of the children's things were confiscated and never given back. Once a schoolmate of one of the girls by chance witnessed one of the police raids on their house and made it a topic of scandal at school, thus further isolating and deeply upsetting the children.

After each such new blow Dina remained a very contained and private person whose grief and fears were kept locked inside. She spoke often to her mother on the telephone but, wanting to shield her from pain, she never told her what the family life had become. Dina was alone, holding the family tight together despite her husband's intermittent desperation and the boys' fierce loyalty to him expressed in open anger to the police on every visit. Still no mobile phones or computers with Internet connection or memory sticks were permitted – a serious problem for homework for the bigger children. And, although they didn't like to talk about it, they were handicapped in comparison to their classmates by having to go to a friend's house or the library or stay at school to study.

Despite many court appeals, none of these conditions affecting the children's schoolwork were waived, even though Mahmoud could not read anyway, and after a back injury exacerbated in a struggle with prison guards he could no longer go upstairs to the room where the computer was and had to sleep in the living room. It was typical of Mahmoud's caring nature and instinct to come to the rescue that his injury had happened because he was trying to help a fellow prisoner (the husband of Hamda in the next chapter) who had fallen into a coma, and he became furious with the prison guards' slowness to react to his friend's crisis.

The best years of Mahmoud life had been when his strength and resourcefulness had made him hugely useful to the most deprived people in Afghanistan, both on the ground and later travelling round in Britain as a fund raiser for village schools and well-digging projects for them. Life under a Control Order made all that purposeful life impossible, and took his autonomy and sense of himself from him. The urge to control his family – all that was left for him to control in his life – led to such tensions that at one point the Home Office had to find a separate place for him to stay, though he missed the children so badly that this was not a viable option.

At one point, desperate for the children to have a normal life, Dina left first one then another daughter with her mother in Jordan after the summer holidays, to go to school there. She found it an agonising decision as they were all so close, but she finally decided, 'It's a better life for her there, I thought, a normal life for a child, even if it meant being without her mother.' She watched a brilliant girl who did well at school begin to miss her potential, but felt deeply ambivalent at the idea of a separation from her, 'Here all the restrictions of her life, because of her father, like no Internet, and the tension … the tension, of course I could see it was holding her back.

I'm torn, should I bring her back into all this conflict and difficult life?'

Dina's immense dignity and composure with her children deeply impressed the psychiatrist and social worker who periodically reviewed the family for reports to court proceedings. But she could also express feelings of sadness and anger almost unbearable to witness.

How many times the police came to search my home, violate the sanctity that is a home. What do they expect to find amongst my children's and my clothes? The confiscated money, Nintendo Wii, Playstation, PSP ... the Nintendo Wii a gift from my husband's solicitor for the children ... None of these items, despite numerous requests, have ever been returned to us. Why? Are my children not allowed to use such things as everyone else's children are?

In early 2008 rage with his constricted life and his lack of hope for any different future made Mahmood again try to kill himself, this time inside a police station after the court had reinstated the need for him to report daily. Covered in blood he was rushed to a secure hospital, and he then began another hunger strike, refusing even sips of water or ice cubes for over a month. With his large frame, he soon became a frightening shadow, in his pyjamas, in his wheelchair in his locked ward. He refused appeals to give up, from his family, lawyers, friends, religious authorities, and would not speak to his psychiatrist. He became obsessed with leaving Britain forever and was constantly on the phone to anyone who would listen, demanding a travel document to go – just go away. It was frightening, no one could reach him, he would stare at a visitor and talk incessantly, but never allow anything you tried to say to penetrate his stream of consciousness.

He kept demanding his wife and children visit him in hospital. It was a long, complicated journey with several bus changes, and the stress on Dina was compounded by the hospital sometimes refusing either to let the baby come in, or to stay outside with his older sisters. In those days, it was visible that the children were traumatised anew, by seeing the state of their father and believing that he might die there on that ward. Despite the terror and tension, Dina kept them going to school rigorously. They were neat and tidy as ever, as though they were living like any other of their classmates. But one of them wrote then, 'I have never thought of living this life, I cannot cope no longer, it is so hard where everyone is against us.'

Finally, Mahmood was coaxed off his hunger strike by his lawyers and was released home on a liquid diet, with a badly damaged liver and a serious infection throughout his body. He was physically quite unready to be discharged from hospital and collapsed on the way home and had to be taken into another hospital as an emergency case. When he did get home, still very thin and clearly unwell, within days a letter came from the Home Office with new conditions of his Control Order – no more telephone calls to Moazzam Begg, his greatest support. He did still have one loyal friend, another Palestinian, who stuck with him through everything, but the loss of the link to Moazzam was devastating both to his sanity and his pride – it had put him outside a network which had given him an important sense of self.

Yet there were always times when flashes of the old, generous, competent Mahmoud came through – in the maternity ward of the hospital, handing out sweets with his male friends after the birth of a new son, a new pride and joy; whizzing along the pavement in his wheelchair with his oldest adored son to play football in the park; driving with his loyal Palestinian friend to take Dina and her new baby across London with food she'd made to celebrate the birth of someone else's baby.

Summer holidays came and the children did not get their usual break with Dina's family in Jordan – she could not leave Mahmoud in his state of physical frailty and acute mental tension. And a hearing in the Court of Appeal, which

Mahmoud was just well enough to attend in part, plunged him into deeper rage and feelings of powerlessness when part of it was held in closed session. Two small concessions were made – he could drop the phone call in the night to the tagging company, and women could visit the home without clearance. Dina's disappointment was acute, 'Seven years of this life, how can anyone imagine we can bear this continuing?' One of her young girls wrote earlier, 'Listen to my story, then decide if you will be able to live my life.'

4
Hamda: From Jordan to Belmarsh Prison

'This experience can make a person become another person ... in fact I think they are trying to make us become another person.'

By autumn 2006 I had spent the best part of a life-changing year helping Moazzam Begg write his memoir of the US prisons of Bagram and Guantanamo and launch it, and much of the previous year getting to know the wives and families in Britain of men still held there.

Meeting Mr OO's family in London was another step into unknown territory, closer to home. I knew almost nothing about Arab refugee prisoners in Britain, beyond the fact that on 17 December 2001 a dozen Arab men had been arrested and held in Belmarsh high security prison and later released on the strict bail conditions known as Control Orders – the subject of the previous chapter.

However, Detainee OO, a wheelchair-bound, diabetic grandfather with high blood pressure, heart disease and renal failure, then held in the hospital wing at Belmarsh prison after a brain hemorrhage, was not one of those. He had been arrested only in January 2006 and told he was to be deported to Jordan, as a security risk. The Home Office evidence against him to the Special Immigration Appeals Committee (SIAC) was in secret and he was, 'assessed to be a member of an Islamist extremist group linked to extremist activity in the UK and overseas'. No one except the authorities knew what had made him a terror suspect.

Beyond that, I knew nothing about him except the medical crisis, which the young man who had brought me to meet the family was asking me to write about. On long low sofas along two walls of the sitting room in West London sat his immediate family, six women all heavily veiled in black, and a young man, who was his son and the only one who seemed to have perfect English. I sat on the third sofa opposite and listened to a totally confusing story.

Detainee OO was a Jordanian man who had been given up for near dead by hospital staff when he was taken there from Belmarsh prison after a brain haemorrhage. But, after a night when his family were told by doctors to say goodbye, and they stayed with him, praying and massaging him, he unexpectedly recovered somewhat. But after about three months in hospital so gravely ill, he was, equally unexpectedly, taken back to prison. There he seemed to have lost his mind.

Looking at the six, pale, distraught faces, as bits of his story tumbled out from one sister then another, and copies of letters to the prison governor, their MP, the Inspector of Prisons, rained down into my lap, I was ready to give up on the article they so much wanted me to write. I would never get the story straight, never sort the women one from another, never understand what was really happening here.

Behind the women one entire wall was covered in a lyrical picture of a sunlit valley of flowers, trees and a lake. I kept looking at it, to avoid looking into those eyes I couldn't read, and to evade the palpable waves of anger against the UK authorities and, probably, irritation with me for my ignorant, literal questions, which showed how little I was understanding the enormity of the fear, sorrow and rage against the injustice, which they felt.

By the time I left, with my inadequate and contradictory notes and the sheaf of stone-walling bureaucratic replies to the sisters' letters to officials about their father, I had looked many times at the silent woman in the centre, the wife of Mr OO, whose daughters kept translating into Arabic for her. I imagined she could see how far any outsider would be from understanding anything, and was wondering why her daughters had had me brought there. It was not the first time, nor would it be the last, when the contradiction of the outsider's status struck me. From their side they thought a British outsider to their world should have access to the workings of the Britain which they felt had rejected them; or that at least once their story was told, especially by an outsider, something would change. I knew it almost certainly wouldn't change anything, but a small act of solidarity might just raise spirits and help keep up hopes.

After a few more visits, I had drunk many cups of fresh herb tea brought from Jordan, begun to tell the sisters apart, partly by their various children, and had grasped the basic background to Mr OO's story. All the time I was observing their mother, Hamda. Her story, like those of the women in the previous chapters, lay back in the acute tension in the Middle East with the return home of many thousands of Arabs from Pakistan and Afghanistan after the defeat of the Soviet Union there, and the first Gulf war in 1990/91. Months later she began to tell it, with her daughters translating from Arabic.

In Jordan, as elsewhere in the Middle East in that period, there were waves of unrest and arrests of people the authorities believed were linked to Islamic extremism. Mr OO was in his mid-30s then and had done medical studies and lived for several years in Pakistan, and he stood out, very tall. He was well-known as an Imam and teacher, from a family descended from the Prophet Muhammad, a man who travelled a lot and had visas in his passport for Saudi Arabia, Pakistan and the UK. He was a classic target for the Jordanian authorities in that period.

My husband liked wearing those loose Pakistani clothes, very comfortable, and that didn't help – they were looking for people they could say were extremists to take to prisons. For months he was gone. Then, of course I knew ... I knew they tortured him. When I saw him, he was partly paralysed. I thought my happy life was lost.[1]

In 1991 Mr OO, fresh out of a Jordanian prison, came to Britain and was given refugee status on the basis of Red Cross evidence of his severe torture in Jordan over several months. His wife, five daughters and one son joined him in Britain in 1997. All became British citizens.

The family lived quietly and happily in a flat in London. Hamda described it as 'a relief, like a drink of cold water.' Her husband's own training as a physiotherapist meant he managed his complex medical problems, including diabetes, with his wife's total focus on his needs – diet, exercise, massage. His GP was a diabetes specialist. Mr OO rarely went out, because of his health problems, but in his sitting room, lined with Arabic religious books, people came to see him: some students, some observing the Muslim obligation to visit the sick, and not all because they agreed with his ideas. In the complex, fragmented currents of Muslim life in Britain, Mr OO was never a prominent voice, but he was known to be in contradiction with the views of another prominent sheikh from Jordan, Abu Qatada, and certainly with the flamboyant extremism of the Finsbury Park mosque. He was known later to have condemned the terror acts of 9/11 and 7/7, according to those who knew him then. His dream was a religious one, of a united Muslim world.

After his arrest that night in Britain in 2006, his own doctor, and another who had treated him for strokes, expressed their extreme concern for how he would be able to cope in a prison environment. 'Even the people who came for him were surprised to find they were taking a sick man, in a wheelchair', his wife said. An immediate application for bail was made, and refused. It was one of a number of bail applications for him, one of which was actually successful when he was in a coma in hospital. But when he regained consciousness it was revoked. Another time conditional bail was agreed if a suitable neurological unit could be found to take him. But it wasn't.

It is hard to read the official thinking behind these refusals of bail to a man so sick he could not possibly have gone anywhere beyond his own home – not that he would have wanted to anyway. Insisting on his remaining in prison could only reflect the unthinking cruelty that was the default response of officials in positions high and low to a Muslim man who the UK security services had listed as suspicious. His experience echoed those of Mahmoud and Mr G in the previous chapter.

No one in authority appeared to take into account that the only possible source of suspicion about him was likely to have been his old torturers from Jordan. Jordanian intelligence officials, like their counterparts in other corners of the Muslim world, such as Egypt, Libya and Algeria, took advantage of the moment to settle old scores with opponents, in the new post-9/11 world in which the West sought all and any information about Muslims who might be linked to Al Qaeda. For these and other intelligence services, it was the moment to get their hands on old dissidents who had fled their countries. For the UK security services, a new priority was warmer relations with their counterparts in ruthless Arab dictatorships, and the human rights of obscure Muslim individual foreigners in Britain was of little account.

For months after my little article appeared – and made no difference to anything – I kept making short visits to the house, just to hear if anything had changed and maybe Mr OO's health had improved. But the news was always bad. Often I would find one or other of the five sons-in-law at the house, having driven his mother-in-law and one or two daughters the two hours to Belmarsh, waited outside during the two-hour visit plus the extra hour or so of passing security to get in, and then driven home. I once commented to one of the men on the long tedious days, and got the unregretful response, 'But, it is just my duty.' They were Algerian, Egyptian, Moroccan and German/Turkish, and most liked to discuss their own country's politics exhaustively, as well as the current grim subjects of the war in Iraq and the latest on the Arab prisoners in Guantanamo Bay. In the background the television was always on, tuned to an Arabic news channel and showing pain and death in Iraq,

Afghanistan or Palestine as the daily reality. It fitted with the mood of the household.

The husbands' mothers visited them sometimes, and then new treats would always appear at Hamda's house – tiny black figs preserved in honey from one's garden in Turkey, or from another, Moroccan olive oil, or a delicacy which looked like brown sugar and was made of finely chopped almonds and cinnamon, or hand-crocheted slippers, or an embroidered mobile phone case.

On the days when there was no prison visit, Mr OO used to phone his wife twice a day, but with his hearing aid often not working properly, it was not so much a conversation as an assurance that he was still alive. But then things got worse. He stopped phoning and stopped wanting any visits – neither from his family nor his solicitors. The only news came from the families of other prisoners, going on visits to Belmarsh themselves, who would phone the house with what updates on Mr OO they had heard from prisoners.

One of the men who looked after Mr OO in his vulnerable state in these days in Belmarsh was the husband of Dina from the previous chapter, who had been taken back to prison after a breach of his Control Order. Mahmoud was sharing a cell with Mr OO when he fell unconscious, and said later he had to shout furiously at the guards for help for what felt like two hours, before his cellmate was attended to. So explosive was the atmosphere between him and the guards that Mahmoud sustained a serious back injury during the incident.

Mr OO became stranger, and paranoid, in Belmarsh, in the months after the abrupt return from the hospital according to his daughters. 'He was seeing djinns, and bad people looking for him, that's what he told me. How could my husband speak about such things? This is not him – my husband,' Hamda recounted.

The long journey to knowing Mr OO's wife, who became my friend Hamda, had begun just as her pain and terror were at their deepest with the vision of a future when her sick husband, in a wheelchair, unable to remember things and in a mental state where even she did not recognise the man she knew so well, might be forced by a court order to go back to Jordan. Then what would he do? And what would the tight-knit family, with all its multiple nationalities across three generations, be able to do, she asked, over and over? Acute anxiety gripped her day and night, dark circles grew under her eyes, her own health deteriorated.

Short visits became long weekend afternoons and evenings on those sofas, plied with food, under that picture of the idyll landscape. Always the daughters were there, trying to distract their mother, changing round her sitting room, making new curtains, arranging a small book-filled refuge for her upstairs, re-painting, bringing her plants.

All the time at least one of her daughters stayed in the house with their mother, pushing her away from the non-stop work in the kitchen, taking over the household, the attempted liaison with the prison, with the lawyers. One took on the general household administration, a second everything to do with their father, a third the hospital visits and complex medication of her mother. Often, almost all the daughters would be there at weekends, and the challenge was to recognise which mother each child in this tribe of cousins belonged to. It grew every year, the 16, then 17, then 18, then 19 grandchildren were everywhere, babies and small children asleep in every corner. Bigger girls who were *tai kwon do* champions, or stars at school, would come in and out, and Harry Potter-obsessed little boys would come from football and disappear to watch films in another room. Asking about the absent grandfather, a little boy suggested once that perhaps he could give his pocket money to a man to get him back. Although they spoke and appeared like any other London children, Arabic was the household language, and the manners, which made every child carefully greet each person as they entered or left the room, were strikingly of another, earlier culture. For all the children their grandmother, Hamda, was the central character. Big and small they were on her knee kissing and stroking her. Often, several of them, even the smallest ones, would stay the night because they didn't want to leave her.

In those long evenings, with no men there, no one was veiled and the sisters' very different characters and lives emerged as they talked and talked, about everything, especially anything funny, always trying to distract their mother from her anxiety as well as her own very poor health. Sometimes she would let someone massage her neck and shoulders with scented oil her daughters brought, to try to release her tension. The loss of dignity, for her husband, but also for herself, going into a prison for criminals when she knew her husband wasn't one, was a theme that never went away for long. 'You know, the police never asked him anything ... never any one question in all these months. So what is he accused of? That's what I ask myself, round and round in my head. How can it be that even his lawyer could not be told what they said against him in that secret court you have here – SIAC?'

Hamda's youngest child, her son Issa, was living at home too, studying for his A levels. He looked older than 17, wracked by watching his mother's sadness and her pain as her own health deteriorated with the stress. She was diagnosed with a non-malignant brain tumour and high blood pressure, and she fainted in the street once and suffered a small but frightening stroke. According to Issa, 'Two people are suffering, my mother as much as Dad. Mum left her country. She left her family. She couldn't be there when her own mother died.'

I had never seen such passion, adoration, for mothers and grandmothers as this. But it was obvious where it came from when sometimes Hamda would talk about her childhood in Kerik, near the Dead Sea in Jordan.

We were brought up in such a tradition of manners, and of respect for them, the mother, the grandmother, to kiss their hand, always to sit lower than them ... The kitchen was the centre of everything in our house – the scents from it went everywhere, and there was always my mother, cooking with spices, honey, nuts ... and love, how she loved me ... She couldn't be apart from me, my mother ... nor my grandmother. If she sent me on an errand, my grandmother would say, 'I spit on this stone, and I want to see you back before it dries.'

Family had always been her life's centre. Hamda was the oldest of six sisters and four brothers, the family bookworm. She was a slim girl in miniskirts and had long curly thick hair, 'so long it was below my waist, so I could sit on it – the sort of hair that mothers love to brush and brush'.

Hamda's husband's mother and her own father were cousins, and although they rarely saw each other as they lived in different towns, Mr OO saw Hamda when he was 14 and decided that she was the one for him. They were both students when they married at 19. Remembering the happiness of that day could always pull her briefly out of the darkness of a London winter and her acute preoccupations with her husband's state. 'I had seven wedding dresses, each one just to wear for ten minutes or so, walking round the women's room with everyone singing and dancing for me. The main one was white, of course, then there was a red one, a golden/orange one, baby blue, a very, very light sort of pink, no, not pink, apricot, blue, blue, and, what was it ...?' She remembered how she used to wear the dresses for parties afterwards, but then left them with one of her sisters when in 1979 she left with her husband for Pakistan and his studies. 'I was scared ... it was the first time I left home ... the first sacrifice I had to make.' In the years in Pakistan she always kept a toe in Jordan. She came home to Jordan to have her babies, and her generous father-in-law visited them in Pakistan frequently, and sent almost weekly parcels of everything she might need, including disposable nappies and many kinds of Arab food.

That time was the big watershed of her life, which ultimately led to the London life, the frightening prison years and the great loss for decades of her all-embracing family in Jordan. When she left for Pakistan she had never been away from her mother or sisters and was scared stiff, though she realised later that her mother was probably even more upset. 'There in Pakistan I was like sitting on hot coals all the time – I couldn't wait for him to finish so I could get back to Jordan – to be with my mother and my family all around me – my old happy life.' In fact the family stayed in Pakistan off and on for nearly 18 years. It was there Hamda read the writings of the Indian Islamic scholar, prominent in the founding of Pakistan, Abul Alaa Maududi, and as a result decided to wear the face veil. Her husband was the first person to be astounded, and the rest of both families disapproved strongly, as no one in their families had ever worn one and it caused quite a rift. Years later, in London though, with her habitual black *hijab* and robe she never wore the *niqab* of her youth.

Feeling safe was the *leit motif* of all those memories of her childhood, and also of how she described the early years in London, when the memories of her husband's torture in Jordan faded in the happiness of bringing up her children.

However, now old happy memories could only sustain her fleetingly in the long days of sitting waiting for the phone to ring and the husband's voice that didn't come. After 20 months of acute anxiety, Mr OO was moved from HMP Belmarsh to Broadmoor secure mental hospital. A new routine began for many more months, and the son-in-laws were back, regularly driving her and a daughter or two to the hospital. Visiting her husband in his dreamy, incoherent state was deeply upsetting and there were always unresolved confusions for her – could she bring him winter clothes? Why were all the daughters not on the permission list to visit? Which doctor had seen him, what was the assessment? Was he on the right medicines? But meanwhile, life went on, and their son Issa, by then in university, brought home the girl he wanted to marry, and although there could be no party with his father in prison, they got married and soon there was another young mother on the sofa passing her baby to Hamda for soothing.

Then, to the family's intense joy, MR OO's solicitors managed to get bail for him, and he was home, pending a hearing on deportation to Jordan. The house was transformed, with his bed brought into the sitting room as he was too frail to go up the stairs. Suddenly everything revolved around him and his needs. Hamda cooked endless soups with marrows, which for months was all he would eat. Gradually it emerged that behind the deafness he spoke English and could translate for Hamda. But most of the time he slept, with his head under the blankets and no hearing aid, and the children came and went, as noisy as before.

Then handwritten sheets of Arabic prayers appeared on the walls – his lost memory could not even hold on to these anchors of his life. When the deportation hearing came close, his barrister insisted that Mr OO come to his chambers to prepare – unlike his solicitors who always came to the house. The frail, confused figure in the wheelchair who appeared in his office took the lawyer aback, and he argued, successfully, for the deportation case to be dropped on the grounds that Mr OO, with his frailty and his lost memory, could not constitute any threat to the UK.

However, after the great relief about their father, the family had a fresh blow. The Egyptian son-in-law returned to Egypt to see his elderly parents and, despite all the assurances of the Egyptian embassy in London before he left that there was no problem, he was imprisoned for over a year by the Mubarak regime. The waiting in Hamda's sitting room for the phone call from the husband in prison passed to the next generation – another woman with limitless patience and stoicism. While she waited – for what turned out to be over two years – this daughter, with another of her sisters, took a course to become a maths teacher. She took her two boys on a trip to Egypt to visit her husband in prison and then once he was released managed to get the family's British lawyers to pressure the

UK authorities to give him re-entry rights to Britain, which he had lost automatically by the length of time he was in prison in Egypt. Tension and sadness struck just when she and the boys were happiest – her husband got to the airport but was refused entry by Egyptian security. Their hopes were dashed, but neither she nor the boys gave in to tears of disappointment. They just started waiting again, and in a few more weeks their father made it home to London and, as though nothing had happened, went back to work.

Mr OO never got all his old memory back, and his short-term memory was very poor, but he did get his old *joie de vivre* and his appetite. One weekend visiting Hamda, I found her husband on a long Skype call to his middle-aged nephew in Jordan. When he'd finished talking, he had a fancy to see an old video of the same nephew's wedding years back. He watched the processions of cars, the feasts, the dancing and in the close-ups of groups chatting he pointed out his relatives, showing which had since died. 'And we are still here', he said with great satisfaction to his wife. By then the wheelchair had been replaced by a walker, the bland meals of marrow soup replaced with plates of rice, spicy lamb or chicken with aubergines and, always, salads and fresh fruit.

Hamda by then had simply forgotten everything about the prison years when she thought she had lost her husband. 'It hurts my heart too much to think of it.'

The highlight of that time was when Hamda made a momentous return trip to Jordan after 15 years, with her daughters and their smallest daughters. Everything was captured on video for her husband. The enormous extended family on both her side and her husband's descended on the airport, in such numbers and with such excitement they simply pushed aside the bemused guards and rushed into immigration to hug her and carry her out like a princess. Cars and a bus made a noisy procession in her honour through the night to the family home. She had said that she never thought she could bear to visit Jordan without her mother being there to greet her, and in the first hours in the family home the video caught her with her head in her hands. 'She's sad then, thinking about her Mum', said Heba, her beautiful oldest daughter, and herself the mother of five daughters. The video went on and on, and sometimes showed Hamda on the phone, 'She's speaking to Dad in London, she tells him every detail.'

Three weeks of days and nights of feasts in vast tents and visits into the desert echoed that atmosphere of the safe, warm, hospitable days of her childhood which she had so loved to describe as an evening's relief during the sad waiting days in London.

Our house was always open, 24 hours a day, anyone could come for our hospitality – this is normal happy life for us. When the Palestinians came after the *nakba* in 1948, we shared everything with them, land, house, food, everything. Tradition ruled everything, helping neighbours, anyone in need. That was what we did automatically. My father always had water barrels outside, anyone could take what they needed, for free, not like now when they must pay, even for water. But this was the life then – busy, happy, safe, all together.

One evening, just before they broke the Ramadan fast that year, in her tiny steam-filled kitchen her husband sat at the table popping almonds out of their skins for her and reciting prayers – still stuck up on the walls – the while. And she, smiling and chatting in her mixture of English and Arabic, finished a big dish of scented rice and vermicelli, with chicken pieces topped with his almonds, fried in two minutes. She had become the mirror image of everything she had told me about her own mother, and had brought her world from Jordan. For the new generation of her grandchildren, for her grown up children and their husbands, she was the rock and the reference of how to live.

5
Ragaa: From Egypt to Long Lartin Prison

'After 20 years of nothing but anxiety, maybe, maybe, I can say I am recovering myself ... maybe'

In early 2011, in a sparsely furnished living room in London, the wife of one of the UK's longest-held detainees fighting deportation was daily glued to Arab television stations, with her imagination fired by hope. Egypt's sudden upset of a long-running military dictatorship brought her an astonishing reversal of political certainties. The release from prison after nearly 30 years of men such as Abboud al-Zomor, the intelligence officer who supplied the bullets that assassinated President Anwar Sadat in 1981, meant there was a new world in her country. Such men, from Egypt's long-standing opposition, the persecuted Islamic organisations, now poised to play key roles in the power struggle over the country's future, were the friends and colleagues of her husband.

For Ragaa and her children with Adel Abdul Bary, once a prominent criminal defence lawyer, it felt like a new chapter for their own 12-year tragedy of his imprisonment in the UK during the legal battle to prevent his extradition to the US. Adel had once been a key voice to the outside world for the Egyptian regime's thousands of political victims, and himself a veteran of Egypt's prisons.

Egypt in the 1970s was a tinder-box of political and religious tension. And on 3 September 1981 Sadat ordered an extraordinary mass round up of religious leaders, politicians, journalists, army officers and many others. They included the influential newspaper editor Mohamed Heikal, on vaguely worded charges of opposition to the President, atheism and friendship with too many world leaders. Across the country

Egyptians were offended too by Sadat's sneering references to the Islamists in Egypt. He mocked the girls wearing chadors, 'going about like black tents', and the young men with beards.[1] Sadat was assassinated shortly after, during a military parade, by a handful of young Islamist officers. A $20 million US-trained special military unit trained to deal with international terrorism, which was on the scene, failed to protect the President from his own men. He was succeeded by another military leader, President Hosni Mubarak.

Ragaa remembered Sadat's actual words over 30 years later, and the chill of fear she had felt. This was the brand new world she had recently stepped into in Cairo University, coming from a simple family who had moved from the countryside to a flat not far from the center of the city, where her parents had brought the old ways of the country with them.

Times were hard when Ragaa's father first came to the city and began life as a trader, so the two oldest of his five daughters did not go to school. His two sons died young – a sadness that his daughters always knew never left him. Home was the whole world for the family, busy and happy, and most fun when the older girls quarreled with their husbands and came home with their babies for a few days. 'Just like now, my two little girls love it when their older sister comes back for a bit to stay with her babies, and they feel we have a big, big family for talk, talk, talk together.'

Ragaa and the two younger girls went to school and then to university. In those days she was a girl in tight jeans and a t-shirt, with long hair below her waist, though at her parents' insistence it was tied back in a plait, and she was not allowed to wear makeup. The girls' imaginative life was fed with Egyptian music from the great romantic divas of the time, like Oum Kaltoum or Najat al Sagira, wearing jewels and elegant long dresses, singing with 20 piece orchestras in formal dinner suits, or the revered Abdel Halim. (It was the music Ragaa still listened to 30 years later for a morning treat at home alone.)

In Cairo University Ragaa found herself doing business studies instead of the art or music she had wanted to do, because her final school exam results were only 65 per cent. She was a clever girl and the results reflected light-hearted years of putting play and fun first, and revising only at the very last moment, while other girls in her class were pressured at home into revising the whole syllabus three times over.

She may have hated her business course, but she was entranced by the new wide world of university. Before long, other girls from her class, wearing *hijab*, began to take her aside and talk to her about how her beautiful hair should be hidden, and encourage her to come into the mosque area of the college. 'I went. It was something different. I felt calm, peaceful in there.'

Ragaa, and her sister, then gradually began to follow Islam more strictly than the rest of their Muslim family ever had. It was the fashion for the educated young around them at that time, she said, looking back. The two girls went to an all-girls Islamic study circle where the male teacher sat the other side of a curtain – and on their side, among themselves, the girls were unveiled. One of the girls in the circle was the teacher's sister, and she chose Ragaa as the ideal wife for her brother. Once, Ragaa saw him after class, in the street, a handsome man with a little beard and turban, and imagined how lovely it would be to be his wife. Later his sister spoke to her about a marriage, and then to her great excitement, his family, including him, came to visit her family. The marriage was decided between the families.

Adel left for a year of study in Yemen, and supported himself by trading. He left behind a very happy young woman, dreaming of her married future and a partner who would help her with what she thought of as the 'new practice' of her religion, which had so captivated her with its promise of purity. She and her sister had begun to feel alone, with a sense of separateness from their family, and from the society in general they had known, because of the new piety they had found.

The sisters were stunned when a girl from their neighbourhood was arrested after going with them to listen to the popular Friday sermon of the blind, humorous, prison-veteran Sheikh Abd al-Hamid Kishk. The girl's family promptly barred the sisters from coming to the house to see their friend when she emerged from prison a month later. The sisters felt scared and lonely. Among their peers education had suddenly become *haram* (forbidden) and her sister wanted to stop going to college – until her mother hit her, and then sat hard on her, and she changed her mind. Another friend of theirs, who was studying medicine, left her studies, was taken back into college by force by her parents, and promptly ran away through the back door. 'Turning away from education was a disease, everyone had it.' Ragaa herself refused to work when she finished university, believing her peers who said it was *haram*, and instead saved from her pocket-money for what she needed for her marriage.

Adel, their former teacher and now her fiancée, was the moral support and certainty ahead for them in their new life, they believed. After his return from Yemen, there was a formal written Islamic marriage. Ragaa stayed at her family home after that, while at first he visited regularly and they waited patiently for their new flat to be made ready. She thought it was the beginning of the life she had imagined for her future, pious, peaceful and happy with husband, house and children.

However, her dreams shattered abruptly, and she felt her heart was broken, when he was arrested like so many thousands opposed to the regime. She spent six terrible months travelling with his sister to every prison in Egypt to try to find him. Nothing in her background had prepared her for the harsh realities and risks of opposition politics in Mubarak's authoritarian Egypt, and those months threw her into a new and frightening world. She learned how, after torture, men were hidden for months, until they were in a state to be presented in court or to see their families.

When she did at last find her husband, he was a veteran of torture, by hanging, by electricity, solitary confinement underground, and then a period of hospitalisation, followed by ordinary prison. When she finally visited him with his parents, he showed them marks of torture on his deeply scarred lower legs – where he would later have several operations – and Ragaa was so upset she simply couldn't process the reality of torture on her own husband and blanked it out. Forgetting the worst things that happened became her habit for the next decades.

No one knew in those lawless and unpredictable days when Adel would come out of prison, or if he ever would, and her parents pressed her to divorce. The marriage was still not finalised through this prison period and it would have been easy to leave it, especially as his family, also stunned by grief and fear for their son, had not embraced her then as she expected.

Tensions grew between the families, but Ragaa, for all her unworldliness and unhappiness, would not give up her marriage. 'I was a stubborn teenager, of course I resisted, it was pride, he was the first man in my life, and I wanted to support him, from duty.' Giving up her idea of work being *haram*, she registered for a dressmaking course, only to have her sister-in-law tell her it was not allowed. Under his son's influence, Adel's father had grown a beard, his sister was wearing a face veil. Adel himself had taken all the family photographs and burned them. So Ragaa just stayed home, and regretted it bitterly decades later.

After her husband came out of prison, for those first years of their married life he was in and out again every six months or so – torture became the almost unspoken constant of his experience, and for her a dark corner where she didn't want to let her mind go. 'Miserable me,' is her description of the person she had suddenly become.

Far from what she had expected, Ragaa lived a very difficult life for a young married woman, living between her own mother's house and her mother-in-law's house, or sometimes staying – soon with three small children – in friends' homes while they were away.

Finally their own flat was ready and her husband put her in it with the three children. But that was a very brief time. Adel left for the US, and then later the UK, and she went back to living between her mother and her mother-in-law, with her children. The tensions between the two families were still acute and made her life even more difficult. The classic pattern she expected, where the woman 'dissolves into his family', was not her experience. Her mother and four sisters were there in Cairo, so she was not left alone with her uncertain future, but her old playfulness had vanished and she had lost much of her old family intimacy when her husband came out of prison and they were living with his family. 'Nothing at all had come of my dreams of happiness with a husband, house and kids. I had just the opposite.'

Her husband had finished his degree in prison and was soon a well-known human rights lawyer. He had strong contacts with Amnesty in those years when arrests in Egypt of suspected opposition figures were in the thousands, the repression increasing in parallel with Egypt's mounting economic crisis. Adel's contacts abroad, his own prison experiences and his legal work for others brought him refugee status in the UK three years after he arrived in 1990. Ragaa and the children joined him with relief, and some high expectations of a new life. 'He really wanted to make a peaceful life for us.'

And for five years they lived a quiet family life in London. Ragaa spoke little English, only went out occasionally, always with her husband and his friends and their wives. Despite the nagging feeling she might never see her country and family again, Ragaa was mostly happy. She put out of her mind the acute anxiety she had lived with almost every day of her marriage in Egypt. 'He did everything, everything, for me and the kids here in London. And I was happy because he was with me … at the end of each day my husband was with me, speaking to me, playing with the kids, taking us to the park – it was the normal life we never had in Egypt.'

However, the summer when Al Qaeda blew up the US embassies in Kenya and Tanzania, with 220 people killed and nearly 5,000 wounded, ended that normal life in London.

In 1998 a dawn raid by British police in white contamination suits, brandishing truncheons and breaking down the front door with a great crash, ended the family's serenity. That morning Ragaa and the children were utterly traumatised. A dozen or so men were suddenly in their bedrooms, shouting for her husband, searching the children's clothes, tearing out pages from any books with telephone numbers.

Adel was led away, and Ragaa, hurriedly putting on her black *hijab* and *abaya*, was told to take a bag of clothes and get into a bus with her five children, one of whom was a small baby. They were taken to a hotel where they just stayed in their room for three or four days, without any information being given to them about why they were there, or how long it would be. She did not even know how to phone her family in Egypt, and felt utterly desperate and more alone and afraid than she had ever been.

When they were finally taken home, she found her house upside down, drawers open, the front door broken and a metal gate across it. 'I had absolutely no idea what to do – he was the one who always knew everything.' After five days, however, her husband came home and family life resumed, without him discussing with her what had happened. She made herself be happy again in her family life and not worry.

The British police found there was no terrorism case to charge Abdul Bary with. He was charged with possession of gas canisters, bailed, and then acquitted in a jury trial. (An official letter from the anti-terrorism police at the time stated that after nine months of exhaustive investigation, they found he and the other Egyptian men arrested with him had no connection with Al Qaeda, nor any connection with terrorism in Britain.)

However, six months later, Ragaa more than once noticed someone seeming to be following the family. Once she saw someone standing at the end of street, apparently watching them. The old anxiety from the Cairo years flooded back uncontrollably, though it never crossed her mind her husband might be rearrested. Her husband reported what she'd seen to the police.

A week later Adel Abdul Bary was rearrested. His extradition was requested by the United States on exactly the same evidence dismissed in Britain the previous year. It had been sent by the UK to the US as part of the great fishing net of shared intelligence in the war on terror. His lawyers began to fight the extradition in a process that soon took on the character of Dickens' *Jarndyce* v. *Jarndyce* in *Bleak House*. An entire roomful of voluminous documentation built up. The committal papers from the US amounted to more than a dozen ring binders of documents, mostly in Arabic.

Successive UK Secretaries of State spent six years coming to a decision to extradite him – from January 2002 to March 2008. After that, representations for judicial reviews and appeals were made by his lawyers including several medical reports, which over the years warned of his serious depression and risk of suicide in prison.

In those family milestones that mark a person's life – his own mother's death, his daughter's wedding, his boys becoming men – he was the unreachable ghost figure for his increasingly bewildered and overwhelmed family. Ragaa could not bear to tell him on the telephone of his mother's death, and had instead to phone the gentle wife of one of his colleagues in prison, so the other man could tell him face to face.

Ragaa, unprepared in language or custom, overnight became a single mother, linked to her husband only by the daily telephone call from prison, or visits when a Muslim charity drove the family to Belmarsh, Brixton, Manchester or Long Lartin prisons, or, more rarely, she managed the train journey. 'In the visits I leave the kids to talk to him, play with him, sit with him, and I just watch. I think about how unfair for them this is – this is only how they know their dad.' For her and the children the security checks for the visits were an ordeal, with women officers touching their bodies in the searches and police dogs sniffing them. They always felt hostility towards them – for being foreign, for their Islamic clothes, for the number of children and the stigma of visiting a Category A prisoner. Ragaa's pride never allowed any of them to show their feelings.

Years of dark depression inside the home crept past, with Ragaa struggling with six children in an isolation sharply contrasting with the family support that had made the Egyptian see-saw years of prison just tolerable. Everywhere she felt racism in her dealings with everyday UK bureaucracy, and the children's schooling began to defeat her. 'If they have a problem in school, I just don't go, I can't face it. I know that if they know my husband is in prison I'll get a racist response, and rejection.'

Nor did she make common cause with other Arab wives in similar situations to her own, although she knew many of their stories. Was it pride in not wanting to ask for help? Or was it just a return to the old ways of her mother's house? She rarely phoned home to Egypt, gradually leaving the family bonds to wither. Very soon she had reproduced in London her youth's tight-knit nuclear family life where no outside friends were sought or welcomed.

In 2004 her mother died and grief overwhelmed Ragaa's usual stoicism, plunging the whole household into real darkness. She had had no passport to visit her mother while she was ill, and it was eleven years since she had seen her, and she could not forgive herself for not being there. Her focus from then on was even more fiercely on her own children and how to make a correct observant life for them in a country she did not know and did not really think she wanted to know.

As the children got older she began to hear about the London world outside her flat from the older children, with stories about drugs, violence, stealing from shops, gangs, knife crime and truancy, among their school friends. It terrified her. Her boys had high grades at school, but she became desperate to protect them from the London environment, after several frightening bad experiences. At one point a benefactor paid for one of them to go to an Islamic boarding school in Wales for a while, but it didn't last. One after another she took most of them out of school and taught them at home through GCSEs. 'But then my husband said about the boys, they have to join this society, they have to know how to cope with it, let them out to go to college.'

One boy she sent to Cairo, to do his university years there and avoid the atmosphere of London youth, but the complexity of the Egyptian bureaucracy defeated him with no adult behind him. Ragaa then still had no nationality after nearly 14 years in Britain. In the five years since she had applied, she had not even got a reply, so she had no passport to go to Cairo where she knew she could have helped him. She felt that for Britain she was nobody.

The exhaustion of the household's everyday work, the weight of the responsibility for the children, the shielding of her husband from the day to day stresses – 'What can he do? What's the point of telling him things?' – took a big toll on Ragaa's own health. Money was very short. There was a time she slept on the floor as the family were a bed short, winters when she didn't turn on the heating, and she set the phone so no one could make outgoing calls, only using it for the daily in-coming calls from her husband. She developed complex health problems, compounded by a lifestyle of being always at home, taking care of her two younger daughters once she had withdrawn them too from school, and taking no exercise.

Her oldest daughter was married early, and to a cousin, arranged by Adel from prison in a moment of effective paternal authority. Her new babies were often in Ragaa's care too, as her daughter, with fluent English, took up much of the time-consuming, never-ending round of administrative battles with the local council or the benefits office, and the hospital appointments for her mother. Stress, disappointment, confusion, ate up every hour, but she had her mother's character and never complained.

Ragaa's two youngest girls were always touchingly open about how sad they felt and how much they missed their Dad. The older one wrote a poem after he had been gone about six years. It was about her 'honey-coloured teddy that was given to me from my Dad/Each time I looked at it, it made me feel sad.' They were contained, well-mannered girls who studied hard, but they were quietly desperate for company, friends, another life they imagined other children had. They wrote letters to their father, drew him pictures and talked to him when he phoned every day. All around their flat were the pictures he had begun to paint in prison – some bright flowers, but most heavy with the symbolism of prison, keys and cell bars. That atmosphere lay over the home. Somewhere along the way, hope of his release died – until, years later, the jolt of the Arab Spring in Egypt gave it a flicker of life in 2011.

In the house no one spoke, or thought about, Adel's actual case. It was too overwhelming, just a great immovable mountain. Adel was stuck – a bit player in one of the iconic cases of the war on terror, fighting the fate of lengthy pre-trial detention in a US SuperMax prison, a trial which none of his defence team believed could be fair, and then a possible life sentence in a SuperMax prison. He and many others were named as defendants in the terrorism case called *USA* v. *Usama Bin Laden et al.*

In London Adel's work had focused only on his own country, and he ran an office called International Office for the Defence of the Egyptian People. He put out a newsletter on Egyptian news, where Ragaa, from home and while looking after her children, used to write a weekly column on women's affairs.

The extradition case would put Adel Abdul Bary on trial with a large number of other defendants whose names were added along the years, charged with general conspiracy to kill Americans and with substantive charges in the East African embassy bombing. Ragaa blanked it out – it was all too frightening to think about. The one concrete thing her husband was on trial for was his possession of a fax sent to him – found in his office weeks after the events – about the bombings of the US's East African embassies. (These faxes were everywhere in the Arab areas of London at the time, handed out in places such as outside the Regents Park and other mosques and sent to news organisations across the world.) This fax – along with the Al Qaeda defector Jamal Al Fadl's testimony on Egyptian Islamic Jihad's supposed Al Qaeda links – was apparently enough for the Americans to jump to the conclusion that Abdul Bary (never named by Al Fadl) had prior knowledge and responsibility in the bombings.

This vast case was the unseen backdrop of Adel and Ragaa's lost family life. In 2001 four people were convicted in connection with the bombings. In 2011 another defendant, Ahmed Ghailani, who was tried on 286 charges, was found guilty on just one and received a life sentence.

For Ragaa all this detail, over so many years, passed her by – she blanked it. 'I don't read anything about it, I'm just not interested. Twenty years of all this politics has been too much, I have to live my kids' lives.' So painful were her memories of the last years that she forgot everything she could.

Then, after about seven years of sad, restricted family life, Ragaa suddenly embarked on a plan she had been thinking about for a year. She enrolled in a dress-making course at a college of higher education and, once accepted, she got her husband's permission. It took her three visits to the college to persuade them to take her, because her English was weak, and then she was on probation for five weeks. She would soon become the star of the class.

Every day she set off in the bus with her packed lunch and plunged into a class of giggly young British women 20 years younger than her. Every lunch time she went alone to the prayer room and waited for class to start again. The living room table at home became covered in cut out paper patterns, she borrowed books, went to museums, searched the Internet and sewed elaborate dresses which won prizes at her college. All her girls appeared in new dresses, bright colours, carefully fitted. Ragaa's English made a leap forward and she ignored her acute fatigue, pain while walking and the never-ending stressful daily background of continuous confusion over benefit payments, the boys' schooling and her poor health.

At the end of the year she passed with distinction and for days was on a high with happiness she had never known in Britain. She was then accepted by the college for a two-year higher level course, although this time her husband told her he would prefer her to stay home.

He also told her he worried about her safety and preferred she did not make a trip to Cairo in 2009 when her British passport finally came through. But she went anyway, with her little girls and one boy. After 17 years she saw her own family again, and got a measure of how far the hard, lonely, years in London had taken her from an Egyptian life, which she no longer felt she fitted. Her family told her they found she had become cold and British, which made her laugh, recounting it afterwards. But the aching loss of the illusion that she and the children had a big family somewhere else as a background resource was very hard, though she did not dwell on it.

In late 2010 there was a prolonged and painful crisis when her husband and the small group of Muslim men with him, all fighting various deportation orders, were moved to Manchester prison while Long Lartin, where they had been for years, was refurbished. Soon the daily phone calls were punctuated with complaints about disrespect, racist behaviour by guards, new rules about phone calls having to be in English, not in Arabic.

Manchester was so far that Ragaa did not manage to visit. Then her husband told her he was going on hunger strike to protest about the conditions and his treatment. He stopped phoning home and Ragaa got her only news of him from phone calls from wives of other prisoners, who were increasingly concerned about his fragile state. The girls became convinced their father would die and spent tearful nights without sleeping, and days phoning their lawyers to ask them to make emergency visits to him. For weeks the anxiety in the household was acute, no one wanted to eat or do anything. No one could think of anything but the silent telephone.

However, soon after the Muslim detainee group returned to Long Lartin prison, Adel's mood in his renewed telephone calls changed, as he watched the daily news of the momentous change building up in Egypt. Ragaa and the children came slowly out of their silent tunnel of terror of his possible death.

A few months before, Ragaa had begun to make slow changes in the two younger girls' constricted lives, by sending them first to Arabic school on Saturdays, where they won prizes for their memorising of the Koran. 'Mumtaz, mumtaz, mumtaz' (excellent, excellent, excellent) said their report cards. Then, after huge efforts, she got them into to an Islamic day school – thanks to generosity from various Palestinians and Egyptians. Never have girls loved school as those two did.

The younger one wrote her first poem, *Waiting for Tea*, her imagination capturing a moment of family harmony, uncannily close to the safe child's world of classic Western authors she had never experienced, such as Louisa M. Alcott, A. A. Milne or Arthur Ransome.

> At teatime my family gathered around.
> All was quiet not one little sound.
>
> Waiting to be served cinnamon tea.
> My Brothers' head resting on my knee.
>
> The fireplace lit the light so dim.
> Carrying the orange cake my brother Wassim.
>
> Behind him my mother entered the room.
> Carrying the tray and full in bloom.
>
> With a broad grin on her face.
> Looking very pretty in a shawl made of lace.
>
> Inhaling the aroma of my cinnamon tea
> How more lovely could this be.

By then the one-hour journey each way to school, by underground with two changes, to take the girls there and fetch them home, was too much for Ragaa's fragile health, and usually her older daughter would take them, leaving her babies with Ragaa.

A new anxiety had come to dominate her everyday life since her youngest daughter became ten, and Ragaa's income support was reassessed. She claimed incapacity benefit in a climate in which the fit for work tests were unjust and inadequate, even before the new government brought in even more stringent criteria. According to lawyers who worked in this area, there was much anecdotal evidence of prejudice in the tribunals, and the judgments were much criticised. The government began a reassessment of the 1.6 million people claiming sickness benefit, as part of a plan to reduce the annual £7bn incapacity bill. The new Work Capability Assessment (WCA) had stricter criteria and found many more people able to work. Serious concerns were raised about the reliability of the tests, run by the French company Atos. Charities such as Mind, the MS Society and Parkinson's UK all raised concerns about a rigidity of questioning that did not take into account the range of problems that might prevent people from working. In a pilot project run in Burnley, before WCA was rolled out nationwide, a third of those declared fit for work appealed, and 40 per cent of them won.

Ragaa was not so lucky. A Social Security or First Tier Tribunal assessed Ragaa as fit for work, despite the efforts of her barrister (a volunteer who offered to help her), the evident fact that she could only walk extremely slowly because of pain in one foot, and a sheaf of letters from doctors and hospitals about the various treatments she was undergoing. Alternate Monday mornings became a painful ordeal of facing humiliation as she went to sign on to get benefits. She did not complain, but her daughter, who always needed to take her there, to physically support her and to translate, came back exasperated, with story after story of casual racism. She detailed the pain of experiencing open disrespect towards her mother, a middle-aged woman who had brought up six children, who was queried by a young official about why she 'had never worked', or why she 'didn't speak better English after all these years,' and which jobs she had applied for in the last two weeks.

Her barrister urged Ragaa to restart the process of appeal again, but she could not face it and began to talk about trying to start a dress-making business at home, and giving up the bi-weekly humiliation of signing on, along with the impossible task of finding a job that would choose her over dozens of other applicants.

After the fall of President Hosni Mubarak in early 2011, articles about Adel's situation circulated in English, French and Arabic, and opposition colleagues who had previously feared that if they spoke up for him it could hurt his case began to speak out. Old lawyer colleagues of his in Egypt organised demonstrations outside the US embassy in Cairo for him to be returned to Egypt. Through 2011 there was a new air of hopefulness in the household, driven by their father's constant urging of the children to use the new political situation in Egypt to campaign for him. The oldest girl left her babies with her mother and started a flurry of visits and calls to lawyers, plans for a possible visit to the prison from newly prominent Egyptians, things which felt like a tantalising new opening of her father's paralysed situation. But nothing concrete happened for the family.

In January 2012 Adel watched the opening of Egypt's new Parliament on the prison television and spoke on the phone to his house. 'This is great. I've seen so many of my friends take their places there. I am not selfish, this is not about my case. I feel my nation now has a future for my children and my grandchildren.' Meanwhile his own appeal against extradition to face a US political trial from another era was stuck in the long, long procedures of the European Court of Human Rights (ECHR).

Ragaa watched the new Egyptian Parliament take their seats too and felt happy for what was still her country in the heart, although she knew she would probably never live there. 'My life, it is just my kids now ... but maybe, after 20 years of nothing but anxiety, maybe, maybe, I can say I'm recovering myself ... maybe.' Then she gave a little laugh, thinking about her reliable oldest son, 'He's a good boy, you know, Allah made him a good boy – for *me.*'

6
The South London Families

'My son has lost everything, his wife, his work, his house, everything.'

In Tooting High Street in South London, Europe's first and largest Bengali bookshop, Ruposhi Bangla, conjured up 40 years of history of people from Bangladesh in Britain and the struggle to keep alive the reading of Bangla, in a world unrecognisable to the generation that arrived in the 1960s. The door was kept locked and from the outside the modest old-fashioned shop gave no hint of the huge library stretching across two rooms of the basement, and the boxes and boxes of books packed ready for dispatch to schools and libraries across Europe by the energetic widow who ran the shop. Bangla language was the owner's passion, and although over 200 million people speak it, keeping the written language alive in Britain in 2012, where even her own grandchildren didn't read it, was a task for a defiant believer in the staying power of the Bengali culture she came from.

This was a generation that knew dramatic loss. They saw their world vanish, over and over again, in violence. British colonial India ended with the horrors of Partition in 1947, Muslim families from West Bengal were separated, with parts going to Pakistan's East Bengal. Twenty five years later an independence war brought them separation from Pakistan, and the independent state of Bangladesh.

Another world in Britain vanished in a different kind of violence 30 years later for the bookseller's friend round the corner, Farida Ahsan, when her older son, Talha, was arrested, to be extradited to the United States on terrorism charges. The allegation was of 'material support' for terrorism, through work on a *jihadi* website called Azzam.com, which had its service provider in the US. For the small, intellectual Bangladeshi community in Britain from Dahka – rather different in style from the majority community from the booming business Sylhet area of the northeast – it was a deep shaking of their certainties in their adopted country. Why would Britain give him over to the US legal system?

For the Ahsan family, the arrival at their house of police officers who took away hundreds of items including computers, Talha's passport and their CD collection (from the British singer Sami Youssef to Edward Said lectures) was terrifying. 'They were weird, and rude ... I was looking for the logic, but I got questions like, have you got any Korans', Hamja their second son remembered. His life from then on, like his brother's, felt 'suspended'.

Six years later, with one appeal against the extradition lost in the European Court of Human Rights and a frail hope in the final appeal, Farida's fragile health meant she rarely left her little South London home above her husband's freight forwarding business. The exception was the weekly visit to her son in Long Lartin prison in Warwickshire. 'I miss Talha, he is my heart', she said, her grief so openly expressed to an outsider that it was difficult to watch.

None of the household could drive at night so they were reliant on a Muslim charity to take them, and once a month was what they could offer to all Muslim prisoners' families. Only when the ECHR appeal was lost, and the spectre of departure to the US was imminent, did they alter the schedule to make a weekly visit possible. Talha's younger brother, who was his mother's support and companion, described their various drivers, 'from everywhere, Kosovo, Panama, Sicily, lots of reverts, and they just spend that whole day for us ... it's so very touching that kindness, and they give us stories from all over.'

Farida liked to look through old books of family photographs from a vanished world with visitors. One small faded album showed her elderly aunties and uncles and their grown-up children. Some of this old generation still lived in India – where her grandmother had been a princess, she said, with a great house with peacocks in the garden, in the British colonial years, and her grandfather was a noted scholar with a road named after him in Midnapour. But the grown-up children's families were by then mostly successful professionals, scattered from Australia to Canada, and many of them she had not seen for 40 years. Other relatives were historic figures of their day, such as Huseyn Shaheed Suhrawardy, who was Prime Minister of Pakistan in the 1950s, and her many uncles and her eleven brothers and sisters were mostly professors and doctors.

Farida's father once had three big factories, one with a monopoly making spectacles, and was an influential figure in their community. 'He always looked after the poor, Muslim and Hindu alike.' She was the oldest of his daughters and trained as a pharmacist. One of her six sisters was a headmistress and her family was full of doctors (including one of her daughters) and lawyers. Family visits to Bangladesh had been an annual ritual, and although Talha loved those visits, he often used to say to his mother, 'I'm British Mummy, I love it here.' Just remembering those words made her begin to cry and she returned to the present, showing a file of handwritten letters she had sent to every MP, pleading with them to look into her son's case. On top was a moving poem, which Talha had recently written for her. With her hand on the paper, she said, 'It has broken my soul, my heart, what's happened to my boy.'

The closeness of the family was palpable. It was there in her newly hennaed hair and hands for her 47th wedding anniversary, in her husband's gift that day of something for each year of their marriage, in her second son's affectionate recounting of their swapping of favourite Bengali film directors – hers the 1950s auteur Satyajit Ray, his the modern Aparna Sen.

The photo albums of her own children's early days showed a safe and predictable family world in Britain. She always spoke to the children in Bangla, though often they would reply in English. Listening to his mother telling her stories in English, her younger son, Hamja, said suddenly, 'You can't imagine how much of my mother's nuance you are missing when she speaks to you in English.'

There were pictures of her two older daughters and little sons on holiday at seaside funfairs all over Britain, 'only Scotland we didn't go to', and birthday parties at home. She pointed to one small friend after another, 'now he's a doctor, he's an engineer, he's a banker'. Her Talha was the most brilliant of all these boys and had a glittering academic career, which was his parents' great pride and joy. He won a coveted assisted place to the prestigious secondary school Dulwich College, then a first class degree in Arabic at London University's School of Oriental and African Studies, and he planned to go on and do an MA and a PhD, probably in linguistics. As part of his degree he spent a year in Damascus, and his father remembered his two visits to his son there largely for the immense kindness of Talha's landlord and tutor, who were so fond of him that they wanted to drive him and his father to show them every conceivable point of interest. 'I was not surprised, everyone loves Talha, ask in the fish and chip shop, the corner shop, everyone in the community knows him for his gentle nature. If he found an insect in the kitchen, he could not kill it, and would call his brother', his father said.

Talha's brother Hamja was a gifted artist, who also got a first class degree, at Central Saint Martin's in London. He had worked as a curator or adviser at big London galleries such as the Whitechapel. In 2011 he won a coveted place on a curator's course in South Korea, where the Chinese artist Aye Wei Wei was to have been the director, though he was not in the end able to travel. It was a much-needed break for Hamja from six years of unbearable anxiety about his brother, and the feelings of pressure of daily responsibility at home with his disabled mother's acute sadness. Talha's imprisonment hit Hamja very hard and he suffered periodic serious depression, which made systematic working difficult and meant he was not allowed to drive. Facebook and Twitter were his campaigning tools for his brother. For years he planned turning his preoccupation with his brother's situation into an art installation based on the books read by political prisoners. He read prisoners' diaries, made links in South Korea and Singapore, and devoured the long lists of 1970s prison reading of Palestinian prisoners such as Sami al Jundi – from Homer to Nehru, via Dostoevsky. 'The last book Talha read outside prison was Kafka – *The Trial*', he said.

In his early teens Hamja remembered being 'just like a white middle-class boy'. Their parents were BBC Radio 4 and World Service listeners, the boys loved 'Poetry Please.' The two boys were just 18 months apart in age and shared everything, from teenage music crazes, 'I remember Nirvana was the first album we ever bought', to later intellectual tastes for Ted Hughes, Chomsky and George Mombiot. A deep interest in Bengali and then Arab culture came to them later. Hamja had eclectic interests and a restless mind, which took him on a pendulum swing from atheism to Salafism, and back to being agnostic. Both were thoughtful, spiritual boys, rejecting as 'a hollow world' the competitive life of barristers and managing directors, which most of their peers and cousins aspired to. They dreamed of lives in an imagined community of intellectuals, of being 'like Edward Said' – serious academics, but engaged with the outside world.

Talha's library was floor to ceiling books on every wall, in English, Arabic and the family's first language, Bangla. It was an eclectic mix, from Terry Waite's hostage memoir, and Ngugi wa Thiongo's latest novel, to history, philosophy and religion by authors from across the world. At the end was a small bed where the boys' friends would spend the night often after long evenings of studying and discussion meant they missed the last tube or bus. That was another time and another world.

The room was his mother Farida's shrine to her adored older son. Talha's school photo, propped against the books behind her, showed a bright-faced confident boy, on the brink of academic success. A decade and a half on, he spoke to her every day from Long Lartin prison and sent her tender poems. Big tears fell down her face when she talked about him. 'It has broken my soul, my heart, what's happened to my boy.'

On the wall in the corridor outside Talha's room is a certificate from the South London Bangladesh community, thanking Farida for her outstanding work for the community. 'I was always for Bangladesh, I always spoke about it. Lots of people in the Pakistani community here didn't like that ... but I don't like tribalism, its wrong – my family always protected Hindus and looked after them when there was trouble.'

Talha's father sat downstairs in the office of the freight business he started after retiring from his eleven years in the Civil Service Commission, spent mostly in the British Museum and her Majesty's Stationary Office. Large boxes, parcels, suitcases, all waiting for shipment, filled half the room. Mr Ahsan and his assistant sat at desks at the other end. 'This is my sitting room, people drop in and have a cup of tea ... all sorts of people come here to send things all over the world, black, white, Chinese, Africans, sometimes shouting and getting over-excited, I allow them to talk till they cool down.' He was a soft-spoken man, with a neat, small white beard, and the courteous manner of a civil servant of yesteryear. 'I made this business as an insurance for Talha, it may be difficult for him getting a job after all this.' The time when the parents tried to persuade Talha to go into medicine seemed very far away. 'Only God knows what is behind this.'

Away from his wife, Mr Ahsan allowed himself in the most restrained way to muse out loud about his worst fears, what might happen if his son was extradited.

In the US it will be a jury trial, and when those people hear the word terrorist, well, it may be a long life sentence ... even though there is no concrete example of whatever they say he did. Of course he should be tried in this country. Here a life sentence is 15 years, and my son has been in prison for six years, which counts as 12.

Talking about those six years he said, 'not knowing anything … waiting … waiting … there is no limit on this waiting.'

*   *   *

The other end of Tooting High Street from the quiet of the Ruposhi Bangla bookshop was a very different scene, bustling crowds in and out of a line of shops selling gold jewellery, embroidered saris, halal meat, great piles of fruit and vegetables. The roads running off it had rows of neat two storey houses, one of them the peaceful orderly home of the older of Babar Ahmed's two sisters. Amna was a doctor, married to another doctor, and the mother of four children. Her family life was extremely busy, and since 2004 revolved round the rhythms and rituals of her brother's incarceration fighting extradition to the United States on terror charges related to the website Azzam.com, which he allegedly ran from London supporting Chechen and Afghan fighters in the 1990s. He was arrested two years before Talha.

Amna, like her parents and sister, spoke to Babar every day, often more than once. One of the family rituals was that Babar spoke on the phone to each of Amna's children every Sunday. Prison visits were a rarer treat for them. Amna's nine-year-old daughter, when asked at the beginning of the school term for a story about 'My holiday', chose to write a careful description entitled, 'Visiting My Uncle Babar in Prison'. Her mother hastily made an appointment to see the headmistress, armed with press cuttings, to give her the context of the family's prison visiting. 'I had to make sure there wasn't any bullying or teasing, with other kids thinking … prison … bad person.'

The little girl's close relationship with her uncle went back to when she was 18 months old, at home with her mother and a new baby, when every morning on his way to work Babar came in to have breakfast with them. She missed his physical presence hugely, but the prison years by 2012 had been the biggest part of her life and she seemed to have managed to maintain the relationship with her uncle despite the separation. Her mother's serene composure had helped, and her skill in making Babar, despite everything, such a minute by minute family presence. Amna's younger children, once eagerly anticipating school sports day, asked her repeatedly, 'Could Babar be out in time, could Babar be out in time?'

Amna's third child, born when Babar had been in prison five years, was named Yusuf, a symbolic constant reminder to the family of the Koran story of the prophet (Joseph in the Old Testament) who suffered slavery and prison for long years before emerging as a revered leader. The family's faith was the evident centre of their life, and key to their ability to withstand the long years of grieving Babar's absence, and the ever-present fear of his possible future life out of range of them in the dehumanising circumstances of a US SuperMax prison. 'In our faith we believe there's always a reason behind tribulations ... and we always have hope', Amna said.

Nothing in Babar's siblings' or parents' background prepared them for the new life at the centre of the Free Babar Ahmed campaign, which came to dominate their lives. The big change started from December 2003 when he was arrested at his London home under anti-terror legislation. His young wife remembered years later the shock and fear of waking to the noise of the police breaking into the house, then seeing them burst into the bedroom in full riot gear, forcing her husband to the ground, punching and kicking him all over his body and especially his head. 'Obviously I couldn't get out of bed, and I was shouting at them and telling them to stop ... then one officer told me to go in the next room, and the last I saw of Babar, you know, his face was up against the floor, and I honestly thought they were on the verge of killing him they were assaulting him so much.' She remembered how she was trembling, 'shaking profusely throughout the whole ordeal' and in a state of shock, and was forced by the police to leave her house immediately, at dawn.

She set out for Babar's parents' and sister's nearby houses, where dozens of officers were also carrying out searches. The first thing in her mind was fear for the impact on his parents of the shock of the violence that had happened. 'My father-in law's a heart patient ... here was actually an ambulance there, so wicked, they even prepared for needing a medical team.' Four years later she still had every detail of the raid fresh in her mind, the detail of what her husband told her he went through thereafter at the hands of the police and the injuries she saw on his body when he was released a week later. 'He had a black eye, his arms were very, very sore, especially near the wrists, he was limping ... and I could tell this was not the same Babar that had fallen asleep, you know, a few nights before. Since that day he's been a changed man.'

She herself suffered from nightmares and flashbacks, and feelings that she would never again be safe in her own house. 'You know, I can't ... I find it very difficult to recount what he went through, because mentally it scars you for life. Babar obviously still feels the effects even now, and so do I.' She was given compassionate leave from her job as a teacher, but she later left altogether, feeling it was not fair on the children, as she couldn't keep her mind in the classroom.

By the time Babar reached the police station that morning he had sustained at least 73 forensically recorded injuries, including bleeding in his ears and urine. Six days later he was released without charge. But that was just the beginning of a saga: another arrest eight months later, on an extradition warrant from the US; an appeal against it to the highest court in Britain failing; bail applications failing; the European Court of Human Rights in 2007 preventing the extradition at the very last moment, after the family had said goodbye to him, and agreeing to hear the case, but in April 2012 refusing his appeal, leaving only a faint chance of a final appeal; two court cases by Babar against the Metropolitan police for assault; an unprecedented award of £60,000 to Babar, with an admission of liability by the police for grave abuse.

Every step of the complex legal procedures over eight years was documented in the family campaign's very professional website. In addition the family managed a campaign of Babar standing for Parliament from prison, as the Irish icon Bobby Sands once did, and organised an on-line petition to have a debate in Parliament on the question of him being tried in the UK not the US. There was no organisational support, but family and friends managed to get more than 140,000 people to sign – well above the 100,000 target.

All this was enormously time-consuming and a steep learning curve, especially against their background of shock and grief. As Amna put it, smiling, 'If you had told me ten years ago that Babar would be in prison and we would have learned all these things about the law, the media, web campaigns, public speaking and so on – I couldn't have possibly imagined it.' Her father, Ashfaq, was astounded at his children's rapidly acquired skills in areas he would never have believed for one moment they would need to go. He himself became the family's public campaigner.

All this was a long, long, way from the family's carefree summers spent in Pakistan with the children's grandparents on both sides. For most of those weeks, Sabiha, Amna and Babar's mother, was back in her own mother's big house with servants, in Karachi. Every summer it was the centre of a world of small cousins when Sabiha's four sisters and three brothers all brought their children for holidays. Amna remembered endless games of hide and seek with the dozens of cousins, and how all the girls would sleep like sardines in a row on the floor, staying up all night talking and talking, fighting with the boys over which group's turn it was to have the one bedroom with air-conditioning. Family photos from that time show restaurant parties with 30 people or more at a long table.

An indelible feature of the house and the summers was the huge mango tree, which spread out of the garden onto the road.

Up the road was a boys' school and Babar used to marshal a platoon of cousins to guard his grandmother's mangoes when they fell beyond the garden into the road where the school boys passed in droves. Sabiha and Babar, her second son, were the mango lovers of the family, and early every morning they were primed for a race to get the best mangoes. 'I used to tell my son, I love you so much, I'll do anything for you, give you everything … except share my mango.'

That Pakistani home had followed the first great upheaval of her life for Sabiha. She and Ashfaq both suffered the childhood shock of British India ending with partition, and the families leaving the great north India cities of Allahabad and Meerut for the new Pakistan. However, their large families of writers, school and university teachers soon adapted well. Sabiha at school was an all-round star in class and on the games field winning medals for the javelin and shot-put, and was on the netball team. Sabiha and Ashfaq were distant relatives, and Sabiha's favourite aunt, whose four daughters had been her friends all her life, suggested Sabiha, a scientist specialising in biology, as a wife to her brother when he was studying in London. Ashfaq said he wanted only two things, laughter with a sense of humour and a nice voice. With the exchange of a video of a young woman on a swing in a garden in Karachi, and a photograph of a young man in London, the marriage was arranged.

Years later in London, they had two boys and two girls, and while Ashfaq worked for 20 years as a civil servant in the then Department of Overseas Aid, Sabiha taught A level science part time and devoted herself primarily to bringing up her children. During her school years, Amna found Babar was like the older sister she didn't have, always the person who would ask her every evening, 'Tell me everything about your day', and advise her on everything imaginable.

For the cousins, spread across the world from Saudi Arabia and Malaysia, to Canada and the US, Babar had always had the same role. Everyone remembered him staying up all night helping one boy produce a class project due in the morning. The shock of his arrest was felt deeply by all of them around the world – for each of them Babar had been the special cousin who had paid them attention, solved their problems. The immediate family by then were mostly living within ten minutes' walk of their parents' house and every Friday without fail they would squeeze into their parents' house to eat together, and on weekends go for picnics all together. 'Laughter and family closeness', is everyone's abiding memory of those years before Babar's two arrests.

The biggest shock of the arrests was for Babar's mother, Sabiha. Eight years into the ordeal that transformed her life, she loved to talk about her past happiness with him. Her gentle, tired face lit up with a smile suddenly as pictures of him came into her head: Babar as a four year old in Pakistan at a wedding, hiding on the stairs or under the table, to get away from the spicy food; Babar in primary school, running home carrying his brother's school bag as well as his own, too independent to wait for a lift; Babar sitting snuggled next to her on the sofa as she coached him through preparation for the eleven plus exam with promises of treats to come. Then, as he grew up, Babar had become the person who was always taking care of her, she said. Sabiha had often been in hospital with high blood pressure. She tired easily from her teaching job, and Babar was the person who bought her a foot spa and would prepare her a bath with relaxing oil, or make a huge dish of fish fingers for everyone, so she didn't have to cook. His mother remembered how, 'he would leave the kitchen spotless for you, as a girl would know how it should be'.

Once he was in prison, the family discovered that it was not just the extended family that had got this attentive looking after. One person after another from the community came to visit them and told how Babar had done their UCAS university entrance forms with them, or done a CV, or a guide to how to manage the Haj pilgrimage. His sister talked of how 'he had time for everyone'. Those local friends spontaneously organised a rota to drive the parents to the prison up in the Midlands. Once a month, over all these years, they were taken by a Muslim charity, but the other weekends saw a succession of young men ready to give up their whole day for the trip and often refusing even to take the money for petrol.

To go from the orderly happy world that was theirs, to the weekly routine of visiting their son in a high security prison, was a stunning shock, which had left both parents sadder than words can convey, or any outsider can really take in. After the long drive, the entrance procedures meant finger print identification three times, a physical search, even for women like Amna, fully veiled, a sniffer dog circling each person, a series of locked doors to be escorted through, before sitting at a designated table where the prisoner had a different colour chair from the others. Visitors could take nothing into the visiting room, everything had to be left in a locker outside, except a small see-though plastic bag containing change for the machines in the visiting room selling drinks and chocolate. Amna described how two hours always flew past in talk of family news, but for the last half-hour Babar, in his old way, began the encouragement of each family member, which kept them strong through the next six days apart. 'My son encourages me, he is the one who gives me strength', his father said. In the early days, Babar's wife remembered years later, none of them wanted to think about what would happen if he was extradited, but Babar insisted they talk about it, to prepare themselves in case it happened. His wife said, 'You have to psyche yourself up for that, he would say, I have to talk about it, because it is a real possibility.'

No preparation, no encouragement, not even the strongest faith in being looked after by Allah could be enough for a mother's heart's response to the loss of her son as he had been in her daily life. 'When I have to say, bye, bye, my heart is broken', his mother said, her voice breaking and her daughter's hand quickly reaching to comfort her. It was a moment of the deepest private grief. Her husband described those painful minutes when time was up and the visitors had to leave the prison visiting room at Long Lartin, waiting for the doors to be unlocked on one side, while the prisoners were escorted away through the door unlocked on the opposite side. Both sides looked back at the other, becoming more and more distant, re-entering their different worlds.

Babar's prison world was something his parents could not bear to think too much about. Though they did have to bear the knowledge that their son was kept for years isolated in a very small unit of around seven Muslim men, not allowed to pray or eat with other prisoners even during the Eid festival, deprived periodically of access to the gym or to a creative workshop. 'He does not tell me everything that happens to him there, he tries to shield me, though I did find out later that he is strip-searched every time, coming to see us, and then going back …', his father's words trailed off.

The most painful of times for the parents were the years' regular festivities and gatherings in their community, Eid celebrations and weddings. 'My eyes are searching for him in that crowd where I see all his friends – sometimes I have to come outside because I've got so upset', said his father. 'Every night of Ramadan, when sunset comes and the family starts to eat together, I think of him, he's alone', said his mother.

Ashfaq had spoken publicly, tirelessly for a trial in Britain for his son, on television, on radio, in meetings, from on a box in the street outside the Home Office, on a stage erected outside 10 Downing Street, in meetings in the House of Commons and in community centres and universities. For the first five years, Babar's young wife also spoke in countless meetings, about the violent first arrest as they were woken from sleep, the incomprehension of what the US charges were, the terror of the US prison regime for Muslims. But later, as the years dragged on and no one could say when, if ever, Babar would be released in Britain, the marriage was ended – an additional cause of deep distress all round. All Babar's clothes and effects were then brought to his parents' house and he told his mother to give them away. 'I would never do that, my husband gets so sad at the very thought of that. I keep everything for Babar, for when he comes back', his mother said.

'My son has lost everything, his wife, his home, his job', his father said once with tears shining in his eyes. He took inspiration from Moazzam Begg's father who, a decade before, campaigned tirelessly for his son's return from Guantanamo Bay. 'He got his son back, and so will I.' In the court where the last case against the police was heard Ashfaq was present every day, and said afterwards he had difficulty holding on to his faith in the British justice system. He heard an edited tape played in court, not the full tape, omitting the phrase, 'Where is your God now?', which Babar said the arresting officers had used to mock him; he saw one juror removed who was a member of Amnesty International; and saw some of the jurors go forward to shake the hands of the police officers when they were acquitted. The jury had not been allowed to know that the Metropolitan police had previously admitted liability and offered to pay him £60,000 damages for his injuries. 'I do still have faith, but my confidence was shaken, I thought British justice was the best in the world', his father said quietly.

Once a year Babar's parents took a break from the stress of waiting with no end, the tantalising contact of daily phone calls and the weekly large prison visiting hall, and went to Saudi Arabia to see their elder son and his children, to relax with Sabiha's sister, and to visit the comfort and inspiration of Mecca. 'Our faith is everything', Amna said often, with her wide smile.

7
Daughters and Sisters

'It's not like a death, you don't grieve, and then finish, because this is not in the past, in fact it's not even in the back of my mind – it is always there … this is chronic, after nine years, and it is not going to end.'

The women's party room at the wedding of a former Guantanamo Bay prisoner was a confusion of enthusiastic young women dancing, small children in their best clothes running wild, and women of every age, in every possible different colour of veil and dress, talking enthusiastically and eating from the buffet of great heaped dishes of lamb, chicken and rice. Above it all, the bride sat on a throne, and was taken out by her mother every now and again, only to reappear in a different dress and to be greeted by celebratory ululating from dozens of throats. Only in London could there be such a mixture of women from Algeria, Iraq, Lebanon, Palestine, Egypt, Jordan, Somalia. And only among this group of survivors of some of the worst experiences of the war on terror could there be such a poignant, rare moment of an explosion of high spirits. In that West London evening, the group solidarity of many women who did not know each other personally, but often knew the others' stories, was palpable. And it was as though, in that atmosphere of joy, everyone had chosen to forget the utter bleakness so many of them had lived through, or still were confronting on a daily basis, with husbands in prison, or under house arrest, or returned to the family as a different man, transformed by the horrors of Bagram and Guantanamo.

On one strikingly quiet table, among black robes, *hijabs* and some *niqabs*, were the pale faces and deep brown eyes of three young girls and their mother, smiling quietly and being greeted by a procession of well-wishers. There was nothing about them to suggest a family living a unique drama and a frighteningly uncertain future, nor any hint of the mother's reputation as a respected role model for many who knew her only by name or by speaking to her on the telephone in times of their own special family troubles. The father of the family, Abu Qatada, a Palestinian/Jordanian Islamic scholar, had become a household name in Britain, as a feared and unspecified threat. His was the only really well-known name among the dozen Muslim men held in Britain's post 9/11 round up into Belmarsh prison (after some months in hiding). He was a favourite target of a British Islamophobic media, which robustly supported the government's attempts to deport him to Jordan, where he was accused of terrorism. And his was also the name that many of the men from Britain held in Guantanamo, including the bridegroom that evening, had been extensively questioned about by the US authorities.

Abu Qatada was a household name in parts of the Muslim community in Britain from the 1990s. He had a powerful charismatic personality, was a prolific writer, regular public speaker and carried the weighty status of a religious scholar. On all the boiling conflicts in Muslim areas of the period, from Algeria to Afghanistan, and those less visible, against Egypt and Jordan's repressive regimes, his influential views were out in public. They were influences that the US and its allies believed encouraged violent extremism and were likely to legitimise Al Qaeda's terrorism. In Jordan, five years after arriving in Britain and getting political asylum, he was condemned in a military court in absentia in 1998 and 1999, once to life imprisonment and once to 15 years with hard labour for alleged involvement in plots to cause explosions. His co-defendants, who testified against him, later said they had been tortured.

Years later at their home in a quiet leafy London road I came to know an unusually united family, at table together eating traditional Palestinian meals, rigorously observing the hour for communal prayer in the sitting room, with the girls and their mother then covering their hair and everyday clothes, and sometimes the call to prayer coming from the clear sweet voice of the youngest boy. Evenings in the sitting room on two big sofas facing each other were for everyone talking things over, or looking through the high marks and glowing comments on the school reports of the younger children. Neither television nor music played in the background of the group's attention. And for anyone used to the noise and stress-level of everyday Western teenage culture, with its open playing out of conflict with family and friends, its pressures of consumerism and competition, the warm, quiet, atmosphere was a shock. It took months and years of visits and outings with the girls to understand that this quiet contentedness in each other's company was not special behaviour for an occasional visitor, but the way they always were, and part of what made them so admired by friends and acquaintances.

Phone calls from their father in prison punctuated every day, and it was evident how they shared every detail of their school lives with him. When visitors were there, everyone gathered together to talk about anything from English literature to the Palestinian peace process, via a comparison of colleges and universities for the older children. It was that very rare thing – a family without secrets from each other. Sometimes there were surprises, like the sudden appearance of two rabbits. The children bought one on a whim and brought him home excitedly. In the day's first phone call from prison, they told their father, only to have him say they must go back to the shop at once and get a second to keep him company – it was a response typical of the family's attitudes to the importance of companionship and family above everything. The two rabbits led a soft life of much stroking and feeding, but it didn't last very long, as they escaped from their cage in the garden after a few months and disappeared forever.

Over the years the girls, encouraged by both parents, sometimes came out of the intensely private family scene that was their roots, to visit London museums, art galleries and a theatre, and confidently find new ideas and skills to think about in a secular world. The years passed and their father remained in prison, talking to each one every day, and they all studied hard, passed exams, got into colleges and universities, made a few close friends. They learned too how to manage their own priorities in a society alien to them in so many fundamental ways. In the British Museum, for instance, they soon found the prayer room, and in one corner the three of them, in their dark coats, long black veils and *niqabs* covering the faces of the older girls, would pray peacefully before and after looking round exhibitions. Outside, the exhibition galleries and the shops were full of noisy crowds, but the girls were far away in their own spiritual reality. Sometimes, visiting a friend's house, for fun or to practice exam papers, they would break off periodically to pray, choosing the garden because the house was too full of paintings and other distractions.

Patience and persistence had one young girl managing, without the help of any adult, to persuade her college authorities to open a prayer room for girls, after a long campaign of letter writing. Two-hour-long bus and train journeys each way to college every day were taken as a routine never complained about. Volunteer teaching in an Arabic school at weekends, or helping out in school administration, were other routines taken on easily, and where other women from their community grew to admire them.

For all the children, obstacles to ordinary life came up constantly, either because people knew who their father was, or because their father's controversial reputation, and prison status from 2002, meant the state had given them no identification and passports – not even the two born in Britain. Once at school one was stopped from taking a course she chose, 'Was it because of my father?' she wondered. Another regularly needed her passport to register in college, and every term had to visit the family solicitor to get a letter explaining that she had no documents available, and hope that the person on the registration desk would be kind. One longed to learn to drive, but did not have the documents to apply. One needed to change her address for her bank when the family moved house, but was told that her student card and Oyster card were not enough identification and she needed to come back with her passport.

Those non-existent passports must have surprised their friends, whose families often returned to Egypt, Lebanon or Jordan for family holidays – even those whose fathers were not able to travel. Extraordinarily, the obstacles, or the lack of opportunities that other girls had, never seemed to upset them, there were never teenage frustration dramas, and they always appeared peaceful, as though the outside world held no fears. One marker of this was how from the class of teenage girls, where the oldest daughter taught Arabic and Quran studies, one described her class as 'like a yoga class'. Other girls who had been in her classes described her as 'the kindest teacher I ever had', or, 'the person I want to be like' or, 'modest how I want to be'.

For the girls themselves, there was one role model, their mother – the secure, still, centre of everything. They loved to talk about her and the home of happiness she had made for her husband and them all, and the focused attention each child had always had from her, the long talks, the complete reassurance of protection and guidance of faith. Sometimes she would laugh and joke, telling stories about when she was a young girl, still unmarried in Jordan. It was easy then to forget the decade and more of total insecurity she had lived in Britain. It hit them after seven uneventful years from when the family arrived in September 1993 and were all given refugee status on the grounds of Abu Qatada's previous imprisonment and torture in Jordan. Before that his wife had had years of travelling, to Pakistan, Malaysia, the Maldives, and the painful separation from her family in Jordan for so many years. For her few close friends, her peaceful self-sufficiency, her dignity and guarded privacy, was their goal too. Back in her original home in Palestine, where *soumoud*, meaning steadfastness, is women's national characteristic, she would have been a community leader, and the quiet and isolation of her London life, unthinkable.

For six years the family's only sight of their father was in the prisons of Belmarsh and Long Lartin, after long journeys and strict searches. But in June 2008 everything changed when he was allowed out on bail – with strict conditions. He had an electronic tag, a 22-hour curfew, no visitors could come to the house unless they had been vetted by the Home Office, and then not more than one at any time, there was a list of people he was not allowed to contact, and he could not go to the mosque. In addition, no mobile phones or Internet were allowed, which complicated the children's school and college work, although they made light of that. (One friend explored buying a caravan and parking it in the driveway, for the children to be able to work there instead of staying late in college libraries.) Meticulous observation of the bail conditions ruled the household, but no one ever mentioned them as annoying or stressful, as so many others found them. All the family made light too of the fact that in Abu Qatada's two hours outside the house, usually spent on mundane household business, he and his wife were constantly photographed by the press, and there were regular hostile and insulting stories about him in the tabloid press.

For the girls, their prayers repeated so many times every day for his home coming had been answered, and the household mood was ecstatic. Even when his lawyers' request to allow him a bail variation to go to the mosque during the month of Ramadan was refused, it didn't dent the palpable happiness in the house. It was striking how completely the dynamic of this family had escaped the sadly familiar syndrome, extensively studied by Palestinian psychiatrists in Gaza, for instance, of arrest and humiliation of the father, coupled with an on-going political situation not likely to change, playing out in family violence and uncontrollable youth anger. The extremely strong personalities of both parents, and the family faith, had inoculated them against bitterness in an unusual way.

The bad times came back with an unannounced search visit by the police in October 2008. Such visits were frequently part of the bail regime and were experienced as horribly invasive, of girls' bedrooms in particular, and, as with all the Control Order and Deportation Bail families, as a general invasion of privacy which was humiliating and threatening. After a day-long search, various SIM cards, papers and videos were removed.

The following month, after four and a half months at home, Abu Qatada was arrested again, and his bail was revoked by the SIAC court. Judge Mittings, sitting with two other judges, was, he said, 'entirely unimpressed' by the material produced by the police from the house, but other secret evidence swung his judgment to end the bail. One of the tabloid newspapers had run a story that Abu Qatada was preparing to flee the country, leaving his family. The family had dismissed it as a mad idea, the house had camera surveillance, and anyway, 'we never do anything except together'. It was not a secret that their father often discussed at home, and with friends and lawyers, other countries where they might live a normal family life and the children might get the education they all prized above everything. Such conversations were a staple in almost every family under these curfew and other restrictions, but there were no obvious country candidates in the world of the early twenty-first century, as there had been in the 1970s and 1980s in places such as Algeria, Switzerland, Scandinavia, France and some Latin American countries which were not under military dictatorships.

Suddenly the fun and the playing with the younger ones was gone, and the old weekend routines of long drives to the prison in Worcestershire, the daily life linked by the phone calls, and the daily prayers for their father's return resumed. Internet was allowed back and occasional visits from the handful of the family's close friends were possible again.

In early 2012, uncertainty came back. The European Court of Human Rights ruled that Abu Qatada could not be deported from Britain to Jordan because of the likelihood of evidence obtained by torture being used against him in a case pending in a military court. A judge in the Special Immigration Appeals Commission decided that the British government was obliged to release him from many years in a high security prison. A tide of media hysteria, strong statements of dismay by government ministers and a flight to Amman by the Home Secretary, Theresa May, to put pressure on Jordan to announce such evidence would not be brought, followed the judge's decision. The girls' father came home with a 22-hour curfew and stringent conditions in February 2012. Their landlord, previously unaware of who the family was, wanted them to leave at once when the media found out where Abu Qatada lived. Any backbench MP could get his name in the papers with a few quotes against Abu Qatada. For instance, Charlie Elphicke, the Tory MP for Dover and Deal, said the decision to release Abu Qatada 'sums up everything that is wrong with human rights in Europe', adding: 'This is a man who is seeking to undermine our country at every turn. It is clear that Abu Qatada should not be in this country another day. This is further evidence of why we need a British Bill of Rights.' David Blunkett, the former Home Secretary, described the European ruling as a 'disgrace'. He said Abu Qatada was dangerous and 'we don't want him on our streets.'

The same two quotes about him were constantly recycled from the earlier years when he had first been sought by the British authorities and later given bail for a few months: 'Bin Laden's right hand man in Europe', and, 'tapes of his sermons were found in the Hamburg flat of the 9/11 bombers'. The family read all this, were bemused by it, always asking, 'Why do they write like this?' but never expressing anger, nor expecting an answer.

Outside the family house in North West London there was a siege for weeks with the cars of journalists and photographers.

The children were repeatedly photographed leaving the house to go to school and even followed, despite injunctions. The children went out every day, regardless of the photographers' behaviour. One tabloid paper wrote a completely fictitious story, quoting neighbours about seeing Abu Qatada, always in white robes, praying and also working out on an exercise bike. It was not in fact possible to see into the house, but that did not stop journalists and politicians continuing to build the myth around the man, kept in prison for six years without trial but because he was considered by many to be a real threat to the UK, though there was no case against him that would stand up in a court of law.

Against all the odds, there were three happy months at home. They ended abruptly one day when the younger children were at school and the police came and rearrested their father in front of two of the older children and his wife, saying it was just a short business of a few hours. Journalists and photographers were in place outside the house to see him taken away. It was in fact a deportation attempt, only stopped by a last-minute appeal by his solicitors back to the European court. 'It was a shock, but now we are just praying and waiting, like always', said one serene girl, breaking off happily as a phone call came in from her father in prison.

*   *   *

Across the Atlantic, another daughter, of another charismatic man born in Palestine, lived a very different, though no less harrowing, experience of a father in prison, and a very uncertain future in a country where her family members have been demonised for more than a decade, but which was her home.

When I was thinking about the fears of Ragaa and the two South London families about what might lie ahead if their husbands' and sons' extraditions to the US went ahead, the Holy Land Foundation (HLF) case was one of those I had researched. I never intended to go further than background research, but then a lawyer friend introduced me to Noor.

Noor wanted to tell her story, was writing a book herself, and had an American openness very different from the restraint and privacy that I was used to. Her deep background similarities, and the sharply contrasting arc of her life to those of the daughters I knew so well in Britain, began to interest me, and as I began to know her I talked about her with them. Her father was not a radical cleric but a successful American/ Palestinian who had lived in the US since 1978, a businessman with his four brothers, a generous pillar of his community and related by the marriage of a cousin to one of the political leaders of Hamas, Mousa Abu Marzook.

The composed young woman in the coffee shop on New York's upper east side was slim, beautiful, with a pale oval face, long dark shiny hair and strikingly delicate long hands. She ordered her food – gluten free – with the care of someone paying great attention to her diet and health. It was not surprising to find that she practiced meditation and reflection, and exercised with Pilates and yoga. New York is the dream destination for many such focused and aspiring young graduates, working long hours with more than one job, including teaching English to foreigners, and hoping to make it as a writer. There was nothing in her looks or manner to mark her out in her society – unlike the three sisters in London.

Noor was one of six children, brought up first in California and then in Texas, from a community where no one left, certainly not a girl, and certainly not to live alone. The family were Palestinian/Americans, her father dynamic and successful, with his own family business. Her mother, who for years kept in touch with her daughter in New York with daily text messages, taught Islamic studies in an Islamic school, where Noor herself was at school as a child. To her, her mother was a 'big personality, not shy, as she says she is … continually in prayer … she left the Middle East and came to another Middle East – a closed environment'. Noor's sisters studied pharmacy and speech pathology, the kind of expected professional trajectory she turned her back on when she decided to study for her Fine Arts Master's degree in creative writing in New York. 'I'm the oldest ... the struggling artist.' All the children appeared to have very American identities, and although their parents spoke Arabic together, the children spoke only some, and that thanks to their paternal grandmother, a near neighbour in Texas.

Back in December 2002 Noor's father, Ghassan Elashi, his four brothers, his cousin Nadia Elashi and her husband, Mr Marzook (who had been deported from the US in 1997), were indicted on 33 counts for dealing in terrorist funds and for selling computer technology to Syria and Libya. The computer technology company, INFOMCOM, run by the brothers, in which their cousin Nadia had invested, was the issue. Mr Marzook had been designated by the US a 'specially designated terrorist' some years earlier, in August 1995, which made financial transactions with him illegal. And at that time Libya and Syria were designated 'sponsors of terrorism' by the US.

A year before this indictment, America's largest Muslim charity, the Holy Land Foundation for Relief and Development, which was chaired by Ghassan Elashi, was closed down by President George Bush shortly after 9/11. Mr Elashi was also a founding director of the Texas branch of the Council on American-Islamic Relations (CAIR).

Noor's dark eyes marked her out as someone very different from the tens of thousands of ambitious, striving young girls in New York, whom she resembled at first glance. They were the deeply sad eyes of someone much, much older, who had lived through long lonely trauma and felt helpless against the odds she faced. The look was not surprising, as after the computer company case came an even more serious one when, in July 2007, her father and fellow HLF leaders were charged with 'material support' to a foreign terrorist organisation, Hamas in Gaza. The case resounded massively within the Muslim community in the US as there were 246 unindicted co-conspirators named with them, in what the American Civil Liberties Union (ACLU) called 'an extraordinary step'.[1]

After a two month trial, and 19 days of jury deliberation, the judge declared a mistrial because the jury could not deliver unanimous verdicts and failed to convict on a single charge. But in the retrial a year later, in 2008, new witnesses and exhibits excluded as hearsay in the first trial[2] meant that things were very different. Noor's father and four other HLF officials were found guilty. He was sentenced to 65 years in prison.

'I took on this responsibility at a very young age', said Noor in 2012. In her early twenties she became the public face of her family after her father received the devastating prison sentence. 'His is the poster case for "material support," they made an example out of my father' (see Introduction on the Patriot Act and the Holy Land Foundation case).

Back in the 1990s, the HLF had already begun to attract hostile media comment and government investigations into its immensely successful programme. The funds went to many causes supporting poor people across the world, including in the US, and among them were community organisations ('Zakat committees') in the Gaza Strip, which were also funded by USAID[3] and European aid groups. The US government, however, claimed they were fronts for Hamas, which is listed in the US as a terrorist organisation. But the family had never expected that phone tapping, searches and hostile media would be followed by the arrests of HLF's leading figures, then seven years of contested trials and appeals, and then the extraordinarily long sentences.

Over the years Noor felt the ripples of fear in the Muslim community, and even among human rights organisations, 'there was a chilling effect, people started to worry about themselves'. Interviews by the ACLU on the listing of so many substantial Muslim organisations as co-conspirators in the HLF pre-trial brief recorded stories of Muslims whose lives were changed, who suffered devastating financial setbacks and a growing climate of fear in the community. 'It unfairly and irreparably damaged the reputation of mainstream Muslim organisations and many of the named individuals', ACLU wrote.[4]

It was a mark of the HLF families' standing in their community that 500 people came to a farewell gathering for the men before the first trial, and daily outside the courthouse people from all walks of life stood with placards and banners saying, 'Feeding children is not a crime'. For one of the appeals a busload of friends came from Texas to New Orleans to support them.

The family's serious brush with the law fell out of the sky onto a tranquil, middle-class world of children's lives, the boys full of football and skateboarding, Noor and her sisters with teenage dreams and stories, and the 'special reason to love' of her affectionate youngest brother, Omar, who had Downs Syndrome. Noor had always felt she was her father's special daughter, feeling telepathic connections with him when he travelled, and when he was at home accompanying him on demonstrations, such as for Mexican immigrants' rights in Texas, into black schools and to Palestinian fund raisers, even before she was in her teens. 'I grew up holding signs.' He was her hero and his principles were what she lived by before he went to prison and through the months and years of thinking of him shut away from her.

My father is my pillar, whose high spirits transcend all barbed-wire-topped fences, whose time in prison did not stifle his passion for human rights. In fact, when I asked him about the first thing he'll do when he's released, my father said, 'I would walk all the way to Richardson, Texas carrying a sign that says, "End the Israeli Occupation of Palestine"'.

She would be beside him.

For all Noor's appearance and habits of the classic all-American female graduate student, Palestine – and her family origins in Hebron in the West Bank for her mother, Gaza City for her father, and Jaffa inside Israel for her beloved grandmother – was in her heart. Once she almost managed to make the visit she had dreamed of, her head full of her father's stories of Gaza and her grandmother's romantic tales of beautiful Jaffa. But, travelling with her mother's brother, she was stopped at the Allenby Bridge crossing from Jordan and spent 12 hours waiting and being questioned. 'They questioned me over the phone, asking me about my Dad, and about the charges against him, they in Arabic, me in English, and I kept explaining, it was just a visit to my family home.' But the border crossing closed for the night without her getting permission to pass, and although she wanted to try again the following day, her uncle told her it was not going to be different. 'I hope one day I'll go ... I must be positive.'

This was just one of the memorably low moments of what Noor called her decade of trauma. The series of court cases had many such moments that stuck in her mind years later. One was when the court accepted an unprecedented use of an anonymous expert witness central to the prosecution's case. He was an Israeli intelligence service lawyer, known to the defence counsel and the defendants only by a pseudonym. The secrecy of his identity was a violation of the defendants' right to confront the government's sources against them, according to lawyers from the Center for Constitutional Rights who said the HLF men were denied their basic right to a fair trial.

And then came Noor's growing feeling of powerlessness.

At first the lawyers told us to keep quiet. My Mom, aunts, Granma – they were all quiet. I never was one to keep my mouth shut, I got that from my Dad. It killed me at the end of the first trial ... no comment ... that haunted me. I wanted to say something ... By the second trial, the HLF trial, I decided I would have a stronger voice – and I would go to the trial every day. Every night I wrote about it, not really a blog, just trying to keep a record. I didn't put my name to it, I don't have that narcissism.

After she moved to New York to study, new opportunities arose to speak and write about her father in prison and the HLF case in general. She did it very well and soon began to get invitations, such as to the 2010 social forum in Detroit, and her small, determined face in her *hijab* became familiar on YouTube.

> I could have been like so many other daughters – go on with my life, having kids, living my life. But this is the only thing I can do … I'm never going to accept that my father is going to be in prison for 65 years.

However, she found it hard and lonely work and was hard on herself when no tangible results came out of it, and then an appeal supported by numerous legal and human rights organisations failed in early 2012. Only the Supreme Court remained. In late 2012 that door closed too.

> It's easy to leave hope – I've spoken at countless events, it seemed to have momentum, dozens of organisations expressed interest, but then it falls through. I've stopped depending on other people. Mentally, physically, emotionally, I'm on my own.

Ghassan Elashi was placed in a CMU in Marion, Illinois, where his only contact with his family on rare visits was behind a plexiglass window. Phone calls were so strictly rationed that Noor struggled in the hurried calls to keep him in real contact with her own rapidly changing life, which she called her 'journey of healing' in New York.

By the time Noor graduated, she had launched the website, Freedomtogive.com, which gave the HLF families a voice in cyberspace, including her writings, the speeches of other HLF daughters and a film of a touching eleven-year-old girl, who was not seen except for her hand, writing, and whose voice read what she said was her annual letter to President Obama, explaining she had told her Dad to vote for him and asking the President to pay attention, study the case and free the five HLF executives. 'Do you know, I have the same birthday as Martin Luther King Jr? If Martin Luther King was alive, feeding children wouldn't be a crime.' In a matter-of-fact childish voice she read from her letter telling the President she only saw her Dad behind glass and had not hugged him 'for years'. Signing off as 'an American girl', she said, 'Come on Mr President, you are the only one who can do this.'

Noor meanwhile had taken off her *hijab*, which was 'an excruciating personal choice' that followed a long internal monologue. And it came at a heavy social price, with one woman from her community speaking for many when she confronted her with a shocked, 'Whatever do you think you are doing?' From a family like hers, this was a momentous personal decision and extremely rare. It would take a poet to convey the loneliness this meant.

But Noor still wanted to say that she was at peace with herself and felt very spiritual and connected to God. 'I trust in humanity – despite everything that's happened to us.' The well-known American writer Dave Eggers, whose Witness series of oral history books brought a number of dramatic untold stories to prominence, encouraged Noor to write her own story of being a daughter of the HLF five. This hoped-for entry into a different world was a big part of what kept her going, so far away from her family, not only physically. 'Mentally, physically, emotionally, I'm on my own', as she put it.

Noor's words, 'I hope my family will try to understand me', were the sad ones of so many children of immigrants in the US where the pressure to belong in a new community is so strong and usually means breaking some bridges to the family past. The contrast could not be greater with the deep family security of the other three Palestinian girls, living in London, but in their own private world with its effective barriers against the uncertainty of their future.

*   *   *

Sonali did not know Noor, though she was connected to her by the experience of having a family member in the special security prison known as the Communications Management Unit, at Marion, Illinois, with its draconian rules of very restricted phone calls, seeing visitors only through plexiglass, solitary confinement and exercising alone in a cage with a basketball hoop.

One day, discussing the impact of CMUs with a different US academic lawyer, she pointed me to a case that was not well known, but that related to Noor's experience, by having a young American woman as the public face of the case rather than her immigrant parents' generation. Sonali too was more than happy to talk to a stranger about her family's trauma with the US justice system.

There was a very different emotional dynamic in listening to Sonali speak, as it was not her father's case in question, but her brother's. Relating to a brother, especially a younger one, in these circumstances was a wholly different experience to relating to a father, especially perhaps Arab ones with their inevitable aura of family authority, like the four Palestinian girls above.

Marion, where the two men were, was one of two CMUs, which were started under the Bush administration in 2006 and used mainly for Muslim prisoners. Its inmates called it Little Guantanamo, because, like most prisoners in Guantanamo, they did not know why they were there rather than in a normal prison. Sonali's little brother, as she called him, 26-year-old Shifa Sadequee, was sentenced in 2009 to serve 17 years, with 30 more under supervised release, for links to terrorism – on line or in his fantasy.

The two young American women had other striking similarities. Both had taken on the burden of being the public face of their family's clash with the US justice system, by public speaking and by running their family websites. Both, as second-generation immigrants, had made a transition into American culture and society, which their mothers never could or would, but they still had a large part of their identity rooted in another world of cultural norms.

Sonali, whose parents came from Bangladesh, lived at home with her mother, with all the security of a very traditional Bengali home, which also included her older brother, his wife and two babies. 'My brother is our provider.' Her older sister lived in another city and was doing a PhD. Sonali was a holistic health coach, offering diet, meditation and yoga, and had the glowing skin, shiny hair and radiant smile of her profession, which certainly reassured her clients they were in the right place. On her website was a quote from Hippocrates, 'Let food be your medicine and medicine be your food.' And on her Skype there was a quotation from Buddha, 'You can not [sic] travel the path until you have become the path yourself' – a pointer to the deep spirituality that infused her work and her personality. Like Noor, she had come from a traditional Muslim background into a multi-cultural identity and into her own individual spiritual path, but holding tight to the values of her childhood. She loved the US for the education, the social life and the learned skill of navigating its fast pace, but the values were not hers.

Sonali's family, like all the others, had each found their individual ways of coping. 'Not one day passes that my family and I do not feel the pain that comes with having our little brother taken away wrongfully.' Her mother's resource, besides cooking everything from Bengali food to pizzas for the family, was constant prayer and devotion. 'Prayer eases her pain, and she finds hope in prayer.' For Sonali herself, her way was intentionally surrounding herself with 'positive, uplifting people, people who know how to stay in balance, emotionally, physically' – the territory of her work. 'I intentionally work to remain resilient.'

Three years after the sentencing she looked and seemed very resilient, but the tears were not far below the surface and started to flow as she talked hesitantly about how the experience had changed her as a person, how her capacity for resilience was less than it used to be and how she used to be a lot more vibrant. Long, tearful silence. 'It has been traumatic, and I feel this trauma living in my body.'

Like Sabah in Chapter 1, she had begun to find the news on radio and television unbearable. 'I can no longer listen or see news like I used to – even National Public Radio is hard to listen to.'

All the family, she said, took their strength from their little brother. 'How he feels translates into how we feel ... he is kind of the buffer for all of us, and I feel he's holding us, and doing an excellent job.' Shifa could email them, and he called the home phone to speak to his mother and called his sister who lived away from home. Also they were allowed to visit him once a month. 'But we can't afford the travel so often, so Mum and my sister and I fly over and meet up there in Marion occasionally, when we can, and we stay three days, seeing him every day.' It is only seeing him, not touching him. 'The plexiglass between us, that's very hard.'

There were months when they did not visit because Shifa found the strip search he had to submit to before the visit unbearable. 'He explained to us that it is not permitted for a Muslim man to be touched, and we understood the level of his devotion making that his choice not to see us.' But they were deeply relieved when he changed his mind and they could visit. Seventeen years ahead was an unthinkably long time. Sadly, but not surprisingly, Shifa's young wife of just a few weeks – poignantly named Happy – divorced him and remarried in Bangladesh. 'I commend her for doing what she thought was right, and my little brother supported her decision completely, he really did', Sonali said. Shifa and his wife were not the only young couple in this situation, who parted sadly, sometimes under pressure from family, to give the young woman an escape from the burden of sorrow and the prospect of a normal family life.

A small group of quality friends, 'friends who are politically conscious', surrounded Sonali, though others faded away after the trial. 'I think people were quite afraid.' Another inner resource she had found was what she had learned about 'several other families whose son, father, mother, have also been wrongly taken away ... these other families inspire us.' Several of those families who were her secret strength are in this chapter.

*   *   *

These young American women, so articulate about the catastrophe that had hit their families and so prepared to shoulder the responsibility of speaking publicly for their whole family, were profoundly touching to the outsider listening to them speak about their experience. As with the families in Britain, one led me to another. 'We're a kind of network of post-9/11 victims', one of them said. Another sister carrying a similar family burden to Sonali's was the much younger Mariam, only 23. Yet again there was a link to Palestine.

Mariam Abu Ali went through her college years at Georgetown University with a big, heavy secret – her adored older brother Ahmed was in a US SuperMax prison, on Special Administrative Measures (SAMs), sentenced to 30 years imprisonment, plus 30 years supervision, then re-sentenced to life without parole. He was convicted of nine charges, including conspiracies to murder President George W. Bush, commit air piracy, provide material support to terrorists, and contributing services to Al Qaeda. The evidence was a confession taped after his torture in a prison in Saudi Arabia.

Mariam was 14 and in high school when her family's tragedy began in 2003 with the arrest of Ahmed, who was then 21, while he was taking final exams in university in Medina, Saudi Arabia. Her parents, highly educated Palestinian-Americans, like Noor's, kept her out of the picture through two very stressful years of the family putting pressure on the

US government to bring him home from the Saudi prison where they were sure their son was being tortured. Mariam's mother meticulously recorded his occasional phone calls, kept all emails and prepared a campaign to get him back through a court case. The family relied heavily on Mariam's older sister, then 21, for much of the letter drafting and contacting members of Congress, lawyers, human rights groups, the FBI, and finally bringing a *habeas corpus* case with other organisations, to have him released to the US.

Ahmed did come back to the US after two years. But to the stupefaction of the family, he was immediately charged with a litany of terrorist offences, based on what he was alleged to have told an un-named co-conspirator in Medina about wanting to join Al Qaeda, and on a confession he had made and video-taped after torture. In court, two doctors agreed that he had been tortured, but their testimony was not taken. And when Ahmed offered to lift his shirt to show the judge and jury the torture marks on his back, he was not allowed to. The prosecution case used Saudi officials who testified via video link that torture was not used in their country.[5]

'I think we were naive then, as we expected his release', Mariam said, looking back nearly a decade, 'we didn't know then how the post 9/11 pattern of war on terror court cases against Muslims was going to be – shaky cases, guilt by association, thought crimes, people pleading guilty though there is no evidence against them, crazy sentences.' She was talking partly about landmark cases against other well-known Palestinian-Americans, such as Noor's father in the Holy Land Foundation case, or Sami Al Arian, the Florida engineering professor (see Chapter 8).

In Professor Al Arian's 'material support' case the government brought 21 witnesses from Israel for the case, which his lawyer, Linda Moreno, called a 'baseless prosecution'. Glen Greenwald, a US constitutional lawyer and highly respected commentator for *Salon*, wrote later about the Sami Al Arian case, 'I can't begin to convey all or even most of the extreme injustices that have been imposed on him.' Greenwald attributed the professor's history of legal persecution to his advocacy for Palestine over decades.[6] Perhaps Mariam's older sister had had an instinct for some of what the anti-Palestinian prejudice so prevalent in the US might bring them, when, in her campaigning days, she always described Ahmed as Jordanian.

Sami Al Arian's daughter Laila, an established journalist in Washington DC, became a practised and very articulate speaker on her father's case over years, as was her mother from the start. But talking about Mariam brought tears to her eyes and a catch in her voice:

> I think about Mariam ... Having a brother go through all this must be specially painful. In fact, I think of my own brothers, and I just can't begin to imagine how it would be. It is different with your father, all your life you know he can handle anything, but a brother, how could it be ... bearable?

In 2003 nothing had prepared Mariam's family for the shock of Ahmed's arrest far away in Saudi Arabia, and then for the unexpected charges just when the family felt they could start to live again. Then came the life sentence. The whole experience traumatised them. Mariam's older sister suffered a breakdown and her father lost his job. 'It took an immense toll on everyone – I couldn't really describe it.'

Mariam said she couldn't describe her experience, but she did in fact, like all these young women, carefully choosing her words to be as neutral as possible, partly guarding her own privacy, but also spelling it out as though she knew how impossible it would always be for any outsider to begin to understand what the family was living through.

The family's second son, four years older than Mariam, became the family breadwinner for four long years, and to do so, kept completely out of the public eye. Most of the family then moved back to Jordan where they had lived before, and where her father had got the first of his many degrees which he added to during his US years in California, Houston and Washington DC.

The family had achieved the ordinary US middle-class life they had worked for, and then it simply collapsed. Mariam, left behind in college, took over and became the public face of the family, though she tried to keep the campaigning side of her life completely separate from her college life. 'I didn't feel very safe, and I was afraid it would have an impact if my professors knew ... I already had discrimination from just wearing a headscarf.'

Very few of her classmates knew anything about her family situation. Hers were very lonely, difficult, college years. She found it hard to share her frustrations and saw how difficult it was for others to relate to what she was living through, and how easy it was for them to be scared into paranoia about being watched or discriminated against. 'It was very, very challenging, a daily challenge – everything, getting out of bed, studying, finishing school.' She studied government and Arabic – the latter was easy as it was the language of home, though the siblings tended to speak English together, but the government course held some ironies for someone who was simultaneously having a personal crash course in government realities.

When she graduated, Mariam found it hard to get a job, though in her very balanced way she put it down to the recession first, and only second the fact that 'it only takes one Google search to find out everything about me'. She finally did find a job in the social justice arm of a Muslim human rights organisation. Initially most of what she did to keep her brother's case from disappearing was on-line, using Facebook, Twitter and a website dedicated to Ahmed. A detailed appeal citing many irregularities in the trial was filed in April 2012, 'Now the waiting game begins', said Mariam.

By then she had friends helping with the website. But, in a phenomenon other women in these situations knew well, one helper soon found herself over-whelmed by negative feelings, became afraid of any knock on the door and ended being the one needing support.

Mariam got her own support when she married a Palestinian from the West Bank who, from his background, was well schooled in making a life against all odds, and in solidarity with a deeply wounded young woman. But even getting married had not been easy in the circumstances when her family had to deal with old friends who had stopped speaking to them and with a certain painful exclusion from circles that had been theirs. Mariam never judged anyone for this, but just said quietly, 'There was a lot of fear in the Muslim community.'

After Ahmed disappeared into the SuperMax prison in Florence, Colorado, Mariam had to make a new pattern of life, dealing with her own continuing anxiety and stress and the knowledge that there was absolutely nothing she could do for him:

> It's not like a death, you don't grieve, and then finish, because this is not in the past, in fact it's not even in the back of my mind – it is *always* there … this is chronic, after nine years, and it is not going to end.

She made a conscious effort not to allow herself to be so affected as to become like her very ill sister, by deliberately blocking from her mind thoughts on Ahmed's actual situation and on his being there in solitary. 'I try to block them … to maintain some sanity.' Instead she thought of happy childhood memories.

Mariam had a great deal of insight into herself and the struggle to maintain her sanity. Exercise helped and for a bit she cautiously tried some professional help, though her parents discouraged it, afraid it would leave a paper trial that one day might be used against her. She did not have the great resource of complete belief in Allah's will and plan that so many of the women in this book have, and which kept her own mother, like Sonali's and Noor's, going. 'Allah is first in everything for her – even before my Dad – and she finds that healing. That is her resource and how she manages.'

In her late teenage years, as the tension around her brother's case grew, Mariam went through phases of being very angry, 'and not such a good Muslim, though I did the five times a day rituals of course'. In those teenage years the anger and bitterness 'ate away at me'. Even years later those negative emotions still welled up sometimes and threatened Mariam's extraordinary public composure.

The family contact with Ahmed was rare and difficult. They were left with a heavy financial burden and debts for legal fees after the court cases. Mariam herself went once a year to see her imprisoned brother and her parents usually managed to go twice. But each visit was the price of a holiday – it meant two flights, renting a car, staying in a motel, for a three day visit of about four hours of visiting each day.

Mariam described the visit extraordinarily calmly, willing herself to share an extremely painful experience and let others try to grasp it.

There's a lot of checking and waiting, then they bring him in shackled at the waist and legs. We see them take off the handcuffs as he puts his hands out through a gap in the door. It's emotionally draining ... he's there but so far away behind the glass. Only one of us can hear him at a time as he speaks through a phone ... I've tried to lip read when it isn't my turn, but it really doesn't work. I feel very exhausted and sometimes I fall asleep in the visit. I cry every time, especially when he leaves. But you know, he's always smiling, thinking positive, being optimistic, asking us about everyone, who got married and so on. He's the one who encourages us. That's the Monday and Tuesday, but then on the Wednesday, when he knows it's the last time for so long, it's very, very hard for him, and for us ...

Her voice trailed off into a private sphere of pain. It was the very same painful experience that Noor and Sonali knew only too well.

Letters were no help in keeping in touch. Letters sent from prison in September took until January to arrive, letters into prison took about the same, and could never contain even a transliterated Arabic word if they were to be delivered with even that delay. Mariam felt guilty that she did not write more, but sitting down to write meant envisaging Ahmed and brought up so much emotion it was very, very hard to put pen to paper.

And in between visits, there were occasional 15-minute unscheduled phone calls home from him while his parents were still living in the US, but Mariam had not been able to add her number to the authorised list, nor had her uncles, or her grandmother, who spent half the year in the US.

'It is cruel and inhumane, it makes no sense ... how is my Granma a security question? It is all to break the prisoner and his family.' But Mariam was not a broken person, just a sad, quiet young woman in a pale headscarf trying to find a way to live her life with the unbearable pain for her brother.

8
Families Surviving the War on Terror

'Truly, I am content.'

The arbitrary way people in Britain got swept up in the war on terror threw up strange stories of life transformations and surprise pockets of peace provided by handfuls of individuals who appeared by chance in scenes of individual desolation, and over years created alternative families.

At a sunny south-facing first-floor window a man was bent over the Eid cards he was making from a collection of stencils of a Picasso dove flying into a pale blue sky, sticking on tiny cream paper roses, thin ribbon bows and signing with an italic fountain pen. Mr U, made anonymous by SIAC, had been released on deportation bail after more than seven years in prison fighting the UK's attempt to send him back to Algeria with its record of torture old and current. In his new freedom he was electronically tagged and had a 24-hour curfew.

Mr U had been described as a dangerous terrorist and his extradition had been requested by the US, after a man he had met only once mentioned his name in a plea bargain. The US request for Mr U was later dropped. His experience with the justice systems of the US and Britain, his past in an idealised Afghanistan, his personality and his faith found in London, touch on most aspects of the lives of women in this book. Above all, the fulfilling life he had made in an English country town, against odds that would have crushed most people was, in 2012, as close to a happy ending as any of the families in this book.

Three and a half years after the Eid card-making day, after being returned to prison for nearly three years when his bail was abruptly withdrawn after secret evidence was given to the judge, he was back at the same sunny window. His curfew was then only 22 hours. And, in a unique concession, exceptional bail variations had been granted by SIAC – the latest for an accompanied visit to a cinema to watch a Verdi opera, *Ernani*, from the Metropolitan Opera in New York. Afterwards he was lit up. 'How could I ever have thought when I was young that opera would be boring – from the first note it was overwhelming ... magnificent. It is an opera about honour – he dies for honour, she kills herself for love. These are great themes of life.' Honour was something often mentioned in his world.

Mr U came from the Algerian city of Constantine, from an unexceptional middle-class family, a happy childhood with lots of friends, followed by a secure life with a good job as a hospital administrator. He gave it up and went first to Italy, a European country that it was easy to get a visa for, and then to Britain.

He was one of thousands of young Algerian men in the 1990s in flight from the civil war, which began in January 1992 and in which between 80,000 and 120,000 people died. In this dirty war there was a story behind every story, and another contradictory story behind that, of the responsibility for massacres, especially in rural areas, attributed to fractured groups of Islamists but reportedly equally carried out by the Algerian state.[1] For the relaxed liberal Mr U, who with his sister every morning would tune the radio back from Western pop to the Egyptian and Lebanese divas Oum Kaltoun and Feyrouz to please his mother, the rise of the Islamists felt like a personal threat. 'The shadow of the civil war and the Islamists came over me – I left.' In a year in Italy he found friends and a job and learned Italian in night school.

This was a man who did not pray. Nor did he speak English when he arrived in London, planning to ask for political asylum. But he had a tiny piece of paper someone gave him in Italy, saying, 'Baker Street – mosque'. London was not easy to manage, as Rome had been, and when his money ran out and he needed help, he went to the Baker Street tube station. Coming out, he turned right by chance and came to the great golden dome of the Regents Park mosque. 'That right turn defined my life – if I had turned left, and come to Oxford Street, I would probably by now have a good job, a family and a home – in those days an educated man with energy could do all that, and I could have had that life.'

When the mosque authorities would not help him, a young fellow Algerian approached him and offered to take him in until he got settled. His new friend was surprised to hear Mr U did not pray, though out of politeness he accompanied him to the local mosque. Decades later he reflected with amusement, 'How amazing that someone who fled Islamists at home in Algeria, should come to London and fall in with the Finsbury Park mosque, and then later here in London with the educated clever circles of Syrians and Egyptians from the Muslim Brotherhood.' For a very friendly person, who got on with everyone, the 'world of brothers' he discovered as he began the process of becoming an observant Muslim was comfortable and interesting. 'I was a very small fish.'

Soon a romantic idealism about a young Islamic state where he could be helpful and where the pressures of Western culture would not intrude drew him to Afghanistan and the early Taliban days. He had trouble initially getting there over the border from Pakistan as his beard would not grow thick and long and his skin was very white. He stood out and was arrested by Pakistani police – no joke when he spoke no Pashto. But he had one of the many miraculous escapes of his life and was released immediately. He crossed the mountains by a long route the second time, armed with a few learned Pashto phrases and some money in case he needed to bribe Pakistani officials.

Years later he remembered with a huge smile the moment of arriving in the Utopia he had dreamed of and feeling that 'something lifted off my heart, and I felt so light and pure and happy'.

Once in the Khaldun training camp in the mountains, with the new name they gave him, he was put in the lowest group for daily Koran study, among Europeans and Canadians. 'A shame for an Arab', he joked much later. The camp rules included no questions or conversations about the past or anyone's own country. The former Algerian liberal slipped easily into a new Afghan life. With no interest or aptitude for a military role, he soon asked to be assigned to a medical team, consisting of one nurse, which looked after the minor ailments of the local people and anyone sick in the camp.

Later he settled in Jalalabad, where there was an Algerian community, and continued his modest medical work, which earned him the nickname 'Doctor'. The poverty and the harshness of life were like nothing he had ever seen at home in Algeria, but it became his life, and like so many others, he intended to stay there forever. It was in character that he became engaged to marry someone who needed help – an educated Afghan woman who was a widow with two children. Her first husband was an Algerian killed in the war against the Soviet Union and she wanted a second husband who could give the children an Algerian dimension to their lives so their father's heritage and family ties could be nurtured.

In Jalalabad he also got to know some of the Chechens who had fought against the Soviets in Afghanistan and later against the Russians during the first invasion of Chechnya. A second Russian invasion was widely anticipated and the Chechens, who had no knowledge of Western Europe or its languages, asked him to go to London to raise awareness and support for them. He went, again being helpful, on a false French passport and an itinerary provided by the Chechens. He was promptly arrested in transit at the airport in Qatar as the passport was a rather poor product. The Qatari officials called a French security officer to check him out. And, with another of his lucky moments, he found the French officer was also born in his home city of Constantine – evidently from a *pied noir* family and took him as one too – and after a friendly exchange promptly ordered his release to continue his journey. 'Chance, destiny, Allah, whichever you like.'

In London he assumed he would find someone else, preferably a Chechen, to carry the Chechens' responsibility through. But he did not find anyone who would do it and was soon engulfed in an all-consuming, and successful campaign from mosque to mosque, raising money and awareness of the Chechen struggle against Russia. Any young man in Europe interested in Chechnya passed by him. Men who knew him then, like those who knew him in prison later, always referred to his selflessness. Soon he felt he had to sacrifice his personal life and his proposed marriage, as his prospect of going back to quiet Jalalabad had faded with the pressure of work for the Chechens once the second war started. He sent some money to build a house for the family that would have been his, and knew that his fiancée would be taken care of by another Algerian there.

Mr U was not a man to voice regrets or even disappointments. His years in British prisons were spent studying, initially for a degree at the Open University, though permission for that to continue was taken away before he could finish. He became a voracious reader of English novels and plays. Dickens and Shakespeare were his companions and he read many modern novelists such as Sebastian Faulks. He lived through extremely taxing years of indefinite detention in a small Muslim unit of men facing deportation – like the men in Chapter 6. He endured an unending series of inconclusive court cases and saw other men with him broken by mental illness, and still others' capacity eroded by depression. His reputation then was as the kindest and calmest of men.

Perhaps one secret of Mr U's resilience was his gift for friendship. Despite not having seen him for 20 years, his old friends from school visited his very sick father in Constantine – from respect to the old man and loyalty to their boyhood friend. The English non-Muslim friends he had made during his year or so out on the 24-hour curfew loyally made long complicated train journeys on a rota system, to visit him for two hours in prison over the next two years, mostly talking over their respective current reading.

Once out of prison for the second time, his old handful of British friends made sure new people were cleared by the Home Office to visit him. He soon had a full daily rota of visitors, structured reading programmes and a regular tennis game with three retired men. And in the evenings he cooked for the retired social work teacher who gave Mr U one of the rooms he rented to students and was the respected centre of this new family. Unexpectedly, the teacher found his life transformed as he made himself an expert on the arcane rules of SIAC, the Home Office bureaucracy, the UK Border Agency's incursions into his house and Algerian history. He was Mr U's obligatory constant companion in the surprise outings to opera, theatre and concerts which 2012 brought.

Every day at 11 a.m. Mr U made his phone call to the electronic tagging company and set out for a brisk two-hour walk, or coffee in a cafe with a friend, or household shopping, all only within the designated area his tag allowed. Every day at 1 p.m. he made the call on the special phone to the tagging company to say he was back. Officials from the UK Border Agency made unannounced calls to the house, checking up on him, and with their right to search everywhere making sure that no computer or mobile phone was ever left in an unlocked room where he might use it. These routines, and the dehumanising lack of courtesy which usually were part of them, had driven many vulnerable families close to madness – but not this one created by an elderly British bachelor. And Mr U, with his spotless little kitchen, his impeccably tidy room, his scrupulous religious habits, rich life of the mind and gift for friendship, was never going to be an easy target for breaking. No bitterness was allowed to corrode his equilibrium. No complaint about his restricted life was ever spoken. Every Friday he called his mother in Algeria, and in his phone calls he kept close to his father through his slow death and knew every detail of his nieces' and nephews' lives and prospects. 'Truly, I am content', he said once with his wide smile.

> Of course there are some things I regret, but the whole picture is full of amazing, wonderful, things and people I have met in my life, where each part, even the prison years here, has led me to great places and ideas and people that I could never possibly have imagined being part of my life today. I am truly content.

*   *   *

The thirst for education was one of Mr U's successful coping strategies. So it was too for the six young Palestinian women in the previous chapter – three in London and three in different cities in the US.

One thing that marked out each girl was their families' classic Palestinian reverence for education. And so the London girls trekked more than two hours each way across the city every day for school or college; Mariam battled through lonely years at George Washington University against the background preoccupation of knowing her brother was in prison for life; Noor took on New York City and a new identity while studying to be a writer under the shadow of her father's 65-year sentence; Laila too made it through graduate school in journalism at Colombia as her father's Kafkaesque cases succeeded each other.

All three Palestinian/American fathers had several college degrees from US universities as well as from the Middle East. 'My father was always a bookworm, with an intense work ethic ... we Palestinians always believe that education will be our freedom', said Laila Al Arian. Her father arrived in the US aged 17 to study, armed with his dreams and his father's life savings. His family had been expelled from Jaffa during the creation of Israel and the Palestinian *nakba* of 1948. They were later among the Palestinians forced out of Kuwait. They then went to live in Egypt where they found many higher education courses were barred to Palestinians.

'For my father the US was the land of opportunity – he believed in the American dream', Laila said, 'And he lived with the moral responsibility to speak out on Palestine.' Her childhood, like Noor's, was one where the whole family was brought up with a strong sense of justice, and closely followed Palestinian and Middle East affairs on the news and through their fathers' public life in the US.

Laila's story illustrates well the four sources of cruelty that all these women on both sides of the Atlantic felt they had had to confront in their different ways in a place where they came to live because of its reputation for justice, education and opportunity. That cruelty came through society, media, government and judiciary in the two Western societies.

Laila's father, Sami Al Arian, was a tireless speaker and lobbyist on Arab/American issues, such as the use of secret evidence, indefinite detention and targeting of Muslims in the 1990s. 'People were fighting ghosts ... they were helpless', she said. From the late 1990s up to 2001 Al Arian was close enough to the establishment to have gone to White House meetings with both Presidents Clinton and Bush, met Hillary Clinton, Al Gore and Karl Rove. 'My father believed in the system, he was working with it.'

However, while Al Arian was having successes in public in Washington, he was simultaneously being secretly wire-tapped and was the subject of a hate campaign in the local Florida paper that began as early as 1995. Both he and his brother-in-law, Mazen Al-Najjar, who was also a professor at the same university, had been demonised in pro-Israel websites since the mid-1990s. And Al-Najjar was detained for three years on secret evidence under a precursor law to the Patriot Act. In that period Al-Najjar's black hair turned snow-white with the stress.

It was a very unusual American childhood we had, under the shadow of thousands of articles attacking my Dad; and having my uncle arrested and offered US citizenship if he would inform on Dad, and his being held for three and half years contrary to the constitution. That was before we even knew about the decade of secret taping of our every trivial phone conversation.

Half a million tapes later emerged. 'What was the genesis of those tapes?' asked their lawyer, Linda Moreno:

They went after him ... the most powerful people in the administration. Dr Al Arian was a very effective spokesman against the use of secret evidence, and he was a very effective spokesman for the Palestinians. I've done maybe more national security cases than anyone – I've never seen such a political case, except of course the Holy Land Foundation.[2]

When the political system turned so badly against Al Arian it was an extraordinary shock to the family. It was also a great irony for a man who had made a major contribution to the key outcome of the Florida election for George W. Bush in 2000, bringing in the Muslim vote after Bush came out against secret evidence. Photographs from that time in history show George and Laura Bush beaming as they posed with Al Arian and his family.

Al Arian was a tenured professor in South Florida University when he was abruptly sacked – during the winter break when there was no one on campus to protest – after Florida Governor Jeb Bush replaced the university's board of academics with rich Republican donors. Protests against his sacking came from prestigious academic institutions and from leading newspapers across the eastern US, but made no impact on the university board, which was close to the Governor of the state, who was himself then the brother of the US President. 'The media, and the university had created an enemy ... the top of the Bush administration were pushing for an indictment before they even had a case', said Laila. Professor Al Arian was indicted in 2003 with three other men on multiple counts of 'material support for terrorism'.

Laila and her siblings began five years of a completely new and strange life, which nothing could have prepared them for in the US they thought they knew so well, and where their family had had prestige. Society turned away from them. Friends fell away, the telephone rang rarely, they saw good friends turn their backs in the neighbourhood shops, they were asked to remove their younger children from a school Al Arian and his wife had actually founded.

Dr Al Arian spent the next five years in 13 different maximum security prisons. The first two and half years, before the trial, were in solitary confinement. The family's contact was by phone calls and visits when they saw him only through plexiglass. Their lawyers were harassed by petty rule changes from the prison authorities. The cruelty carried lower down the pay scale in prison. Al Arian was shackled with his hands behind him when going to see his lawyers and had to carry his legal papers on his back as the warders refused to help him.

In this scene of overwhelming stress, Laila's mother sought to shield her younger daughter, nine-year-old Lama, and sent her to live in Egypt with her grandmother and other family members on both sides.[3] It was the same short-term solution to the prospect of a child having to face so much more emotional pressure from the system than they could be expected to manage, as Dina sought for her daughters in Chapter 3, with much soul-searching and heartbreak. Lama grew up to be a young woman torn between the two cultures of America and Egypt and went on to study journalism at college in the US like her sister.

Looking back, Laila said, 'I can't imagine being a child going through that … it was just such a very tough time. At least I was a senior in college and a bit more able to confront what was happening.' She confronted it by concluding that the US system was very flawed – 'there just are two systems of justice, depending on your ethnicity'. The personal experience of trauma, disappointment, injustice, seen in that political framework, was no less painful, but she had made it comprehensible for herself: 'Articulate Palestinians threaten powerful people.'

Laila also made use of the tools of counselling, which she found a helpful release for emotions too raw to expose to even the best of friends. Very few other women in this book were able to access such professional help successfully – often because the cultural gulf was just too great for the Western professional to bridge. As one of those in London put it, 'Those doctors and counsellors seemed nice people, but they did not understand anything about us – our lives, our faith, our culture. It was useless speaking.' And another underlined the same point, 'These doctors are well-meaning and they listen, but they don't understand that they don't understand … us, and our lives.'

Memory gaps, both current and past, were something Laila mentioned as a disorientating phenomenon. 'There must be a link to trauma, I'm quite sure from my experience.' Almost every woman in every chapter spoke about suffering memory loss. Sometimes they had forgotten whole chunks of time when their husbands were in prison and they were under the strain of shielding both their children and their own mothers from what they were living through. Sometimes they forgot day to day things, from the accumulated fatigue of negotiating an unfamiliar society's rules and language for themselves and their children without support, or like Laila, from the sheer stress of dealing with a world in which a young lifetime of expectations had been abruptly up-ended. For all of them, something worse than their very worst nightmares had come true.

Laila's love of journalism had taken root early on and she stuck to believing it could be an important force for good, despite the experience of seeing the ugly media onslaught on her father over years. When her father received death threats, at the university and on his home email, Laila had thought, with a chill, of Rwanda. As a good student of journalism she knew about the use of media in propagating hate during the Rwandan genocide. Over 800,000 people were killed in months in 1994 and it took nearly a decade before three executives of the private station Radio Television Libre Mille Collines were sentenced to life or 35-year sentences by a UN tribunal. Laila was thinking about only one person – her father.

There were moments in this long family nightmare when America showed itself to Laila at its reassuring best. A jury acquitted her father of all conspiracy charges after a six-month trial. 'They tried to scare the jury, but they failed', said Linda Moreno. 'Juries give up their time, their work, etc. and they want to be there to try a crime. They just didn't like it when they found there was no crime, it was all about Dr Al Arian's speech.' His defence team chose not to cross-examine the 70 witnesses brought by the government, they offered no defence witnesses and no defence except the US Constitution. However, although he was found not guilty, Laila's father did not get out of prison.

In the highly politicised US judicial system, prosecutors were still after Al Arian, even after he agreed a plea bargain on the minor affair of filling in an immigration form for a visiting British scholar, and agreed to be deported to Egypt. 'We spent months on plea negotiations with Washington after we won – as always the government would not admit defeat. In the 100s of jury trials I've done, I've never seen a case like this – they really threw the rule book out of the window', said Linda Moreno. 'Anything can happen.' It did.

The family moved everything to Egypt in preparation for deportation, but then Al Arian was kept in prison on a contempt charge, for refusing to appear as a witness in an unrelated case – contrary to the terms of the plea bargain. He was later released on bail to Laila and put under house arrest in Washington DC – a Sisyphean effort for a material support case, his lawyer noted drily. And for Laila, 'It was an amazing blessing ... having him home was good for us all, just being together. We learned to live not knowing what each day would bring, but taking each day as precious.'

The closeness of the Al Arian family held all of them from breaking down, but the sense of abandonment by people she had known all her life wounded Laila deeply. She tried hard not to dwell on the 'very, very painful episodes' of exclusion. 'My own friends avoided talking about it to me – and it doesn't make it any easier to bear even if you tell yourself that it's probably just because they don't know how to deal with this level of pain.' Laila was good at transmitting both the detail and the overwhelming nature of the experience she had had and was still living inside, 'I've been living in a kind of limbo since this whole thing began ... it defines who you are ... if I'm not invited to a party, say, it's because I'm a downer.'

Her graduate student years in New York were dominated by the intensity of the experience she was having with her father's situation. 'You question everything, even your faith, maybe that is how you learn to make choices, define yourself, learn who you are. I went through many things, even doubts about the *hijab*, while keeping it on. All this makes you stronger.' Then she added, thinking about how she had been changed, 'maybe more cynical too'.

Apart from doctor's appointments, Sami Al Arian was only permitted to leave his apartment twice in three years – for his daughters' weddings.

In 2007 he could not attend my brother's wedding, so I didn't really expect he would attend mine. Of course having my father at my wedding was a dream come true ... but you know, after everything we've been through, having a wedding party was not a priority ... those things tend to lose their significance when you've experienced adversity of that sort.

She smiled, but a bit sadly, at the thought of the classic Palestinian wedding, which is a highly significant and theatrical community occasion, with the groom on a horse and dancing and feasting for days. 'Mine was nothing like that, small – just family and friends.'

Thinking for a moment about the future and about Palestine Laila said how much she would want to take her children, when she had them, to see where they came from. She visited for the last time in 1998, without any problem. But then her brother tried to make a visit there a little later and found himself, just like Noor in the previous chapter, at the border undergoing a surreal interrogation over the phone about his father and then being rejected for entry. 'That's partly why I don't go – salt on the wound.'

After all these years of living in limbo – while nonetheless getting a good degree and holding down a challenging job – Laila said she did not think of leaving America, if her father was finally deported to Egypt. She and her husband had the prestigious careers, in academia and media, which her Palestinian grandfather had given his life savings to his son for him to have in the US. Perhaps she was keeping faith with the patriarch's dreams. Or perhaps the American side of her identity was strong enough to keep her fighting for the US Constitution, which had been the successful lynchpin of her father's defence in court.

On the other side of the Atlantic there were women in this book who had experienced so much suffering from British society and media in a decade or so of the war on terror that they took refuge in the dream of leaving forever and going home to a Muslim country. None of them had the advantage of the prestige in parts of mainstream society that Laila's family had – despite everything. Towards the end of that decade some went home and built another life, refusing any contact or thought of the past pain. One gave up a good job in London and went boldly and successfully to a new continent, closing the door on part of her family and the 'Mr Selfish' she had worked quietly for during the years when he was in prison. She was like another strong woman who had sacrificed her own professional life for campaigning she hated doing, and which she did for her mother's sake, but a decade later was estranged from the brother she had worked for. 'I never wanted my own daughter to have her life, like mine, scarred by pain and fear and not knowing what has happened to a family member.'

Some women went away, determined to make a new family life in a Muslim country, but returned, reluctantly, because their children had become embedded in a Western society over a decade and, although they felt angry and disrespected, they were too used to it to manage the transition. Some went and came back, and then went again. Families split across continents as the political impact of the Arab Spring gave some a chance to go home to a country very different from the one they had left, but not everyone in the family had the strength to go and try something new. Josephine in Chapter 3 was one of those who sometimes dreamed of a different life – in the Africa of her childhood. But she had a realistic hold on the happiness she had made with her children in London and that transcended her daily reality of wheelchairs, electronic tabs, the rules of Control Orders.

One ready to go was Heba – a woman I had met years before among the women with their black *hijabs* and *abayas* at Bisher al Rawi's wedding. She was now ready to go home to a sister she had not seen for more than 20 years. She was finished with London for the second time, she said. The first time, Heba was 30 when she went quietly from London to Peshawar with her husband and children to find a new life, and years later in London spoke of how much she had loved her life in Pakistan and Afghanistan. 'I really loved it. It was my best time in my life … it reminded me of back home. And life had a pattern there, which was really good, sleep early, wake early, no one looking at you, like they do in London. I had friends from Morocco, Tunisia, Algeria, Egypt, America, Britain …'

Other women too, back in Britain, described their Afghan years as the best time in their lives, and remembered 'a sense of freedom', and of belonging to a rich and diverse community from many countries.[4] When things went wrong and husbands were wounded, as often happened during the war, women cooked for each other, looked after each other's children, slipped into the mode of the extended families that they had left so far away. 'The life was not easy, but it was beautiful. We never intended to come back.'

Another woman with happy Afghan memories and the great resilience that marks most of these women survivors of the war on terror was Zeynab, a British/Palestinian from Birmingham. Zeynab was a friend of Zinnira from Chapter 2, who also went to live in Kabul, after the war, in the early Taliban days. She too discovered, like Heba, an international community she loved – though these were idealistic aid workers who had come to build a new country, not the fighters of the earlier period. 'I got to know them all from many places – in fact they became my family.'

However, the dream of contributing to this new country did not last long for these women. After 9/11, the US bombing of Kabul made them flee with their children to Pakistan.

Leaving there, in a group of women and children – all of us in the same situation after the US bombing started, was actually the best time of my life, believe me. I felt closer to God, if you can understand me. I was stronger as a person after that. Of course there was no electricity, no water to make *Dua* (prayers), and we were lucky to find food. We slept underground at night, in sort of bunkers, and we had to make sure the kids went to the toilet first, there was no coming out at night. Then, when we got to Pakistan and were all kept together in one place, I remember hearing one sister, talking on the phone to her Mum and just telling lies – 'everything's fine, yes, the noise of voices is because I've got guests, don't worry, everything's fine'. Of course it wasn't fine, we had no idea what was happening to us, and we didn't know where our husbands were. But what's the point of telling your Mum – how could she understand?

It was the same instinct of so many of these women, over and over again, shielding their mothers, as they shielded their children and their husbands, from the harsh reality that had become theirs when the war on terror touched them.

Heba had come back to London, like several other women in the book, when the politics changed in Pakistan after the defeat of the Soviet Union. By 2010 she was living in London in an orderly house, a living room lined with religious books in Arabic and children's homework or exam revision on the table. For years she had schooled her children at home with private teachers, because she found British schools too easy going and lacking discipline. As in so many of the homes I had come to know, the children's good manners, the girls' gentleness and helpfulness to their mother, was striking. The children got good exam results, but when it came time for them to go to college, and then university, more than one gave up because of harassment or racism. The incidents ranged from saucepans and stones through the windows of the house, and pieces of pork spread on their car, to exclusion from school outings or being disallowed from accepting prizes they had won. No bitterness was ever shown to an outsider, anger was hidden. But as Heba said, 'All the children are affected.' Fear was always a subtext. The curtains of Heba's living room were always closed against prying eyes, the front door had a second one inside and there was a camera prominent on the wall outside.

In 2012 Britain was caught up in a summer whirl of nationalism around a four-day party celebrating 60 years of the reign of Queen Elizabeth and the celebration of hosting the Olympics in London. There was little space for thinking about a handful of foreign individuals and the tragic outcome of their respective acceptances as refugees in the very different Britain of 20 years before.

These were the months when, as a result of the ECHR ruling in favour of extradition to the US for several of these men, families in agony crossed paths in a prison visiting line every weekend. Ragaa, from Egypt, described in Chapter 5, sent off half her family in turns for the long drive to Long Lartin to spend two hours talking with the father they still hoped a miraculous change of heart by Britain would save from standing trial in the US. In a last-minute desperate initiative, an Egyptian MP, who was also a lawyer, came to Britain and was able to visit his friend from decades back, in prison. The MP, Nizar Ghurab, met British MPs and lawyers and made some last-minute efforts to stop the extradition. The upheaval of Egypt's political system had finally touched this prisoner's life. The family watched on television the newly elected President dedicate himself to work for the freedom of the blind Sheikh Omar Abdel-Rahman in prison in the US and all other Egyptian prisoners held abroad, and felt a new support. Adel Abdul Bary was not British, and his 12 years in British prisons had not made him a household name, like Abu Qatada. There was barely any knowledge of his case in Britain and little support for the family. He had been a forgotten prisoner in Britain, and Ragaa a forgotten wife.

On behalf of the British families in Chapter 6 an *ad hoc* pressure group sprang up in those summer months to organise meetings, demonstrations and newspaper advertisements linking their proposed extraditions with those of two other British men, Gary McKinnon and Richard O'Dwyer, wanted in very different, but Internet related, cases. 'British justice for British citizens' was the slogan, and it did garner new support from non-Muslims who had never known that the young Muslim men had been in prison in the UK for six and eight years respectively, facing no charges in Britain, but fighting extradition to the US.

However, the last appeal against extradition for these two and three other Muslim men, to the Grand Chamber of the European Court of Human Rights, failed despite support from the UN Rapporteur on Human Rights, Juan Mendez, 26 US legal and human rights groups and 120 US academic lawyers for the men's contention that they faced inhuman prison conditions in the US. For the wives and mothers, everything they knew about these conditions of isolation – food given through a slot in the door, exercise alone in a cage in a concrete pit – was too painful to think about.

Immediately after the ECHR result their lawyers launched new appeal proceedings in London on various grounds of ill health and new evidence. In a roller-coaster of emotion the families felt a small sliver of hope again. There were two frantic days of hearings in the High Court in London, with several of Britain's best-known lawyers appearing for the men. Ragaa's husband and the two South London British men had their cases bracketed together with the two others, including Abu Hamza al Masri – the British government and media stereotype for muslim extremism. The appeals were refused.

In the end it was no surprise to the families or the men's lawyers and a mood of resignation took hold in the last few days. It was a different atmosphere in the homes from six months earlier when several had expected the ECHR to rule in the men's favour against the extraditions, and all were deeply cast down.

This time the tone of the High Court, as of the government and media, was unmistakeable. The families had all heard that two US planes had arrived at a British military airport three days before the judgment was due, and all formalities were finalised before the Friday afternoon reading of it in court by the judge.

Only the day before, the families had met each other again in the prison's visiting hall. All of them left in the late afternoon carrying heavy plastic bags of their husbands', sons' and fathers' possessions. There were books, papers, some farewell letters to post to friends, small personal things with which a man had made a cell a home for so many years, clothes, even his duvet. It was the last goodbye.

As usual, the children were as dignified and contained as their parents and tears came only in private. Older boys had prepared themselves for months and visibly stepped into a new responsibility for their mothers and sisters. One child spoke for several others when she said that now loyalty and duty to her absent father meant excelling at school and remembering to be happy.

On the day of the judgment children stayed home from school and some briefly watched on television how their fathers had become public property, with demonstrations outside the court in favour of them, clashing with others who wanted them gone. The full judgment was on line within minutes, to save and read another sad day.

Only then did the enormous change in their own lives really begin to hit home – instead of at least one daily phone call from prison, their lawyers had told them there would be one phone call a month, of just 15 minutes, and only the mother would be able to speak. As Ragaa put it, 'Fifteen minutes once a month … when all these years he was next to me every day.' Prayer time was the only comfort to count on.

Ragaa's husband and the other four men were flown out to US prisons a few hours later on 5 October 2012. It was 20 years since her life in Britain began, and for more than half of those years it had been a life with her husband in prison.

In the early summer, Judge Mittings in SIAC had again refused bail to Abu Qatada, on the basis of secret evidence. He agreed with the Home Office solicitor who said the heavy duties of the police around the security of the Olympics meant that they could not simultaneously ensure that Abu Qatada would not abscond. The judge, a worldly and experienced man in terrorism cases, was told that what he called 'sinister forces' were preparing to spring from 22-hour-a-day house arrest in a suburban London street a tall distinctive man wearing an electronic tag, with five children and a wife. Because some *jihadis* in North Africa, Gaza and Pakistan had periodically offered to swap their Western hostages for Abu Qatada, some may have dreamed that this could happen, but it had no basis in reality. For anyone who knew the dignified united family, it seemed ridiculous.

In the hysterical and xenophobic mood of the times no one pointed this out publicly. These families knew by then that the refugee's right to safety did not apply to them, their human rights to family life, privacy, education, were not safe-guarded as they were for other families. Britain for them was a place of double standards, its government and security services tightly knit with the US, and allies such as Jordan, so that none of these individuals could win justice against the system and the media, which buttressed it. Nonetheless, successful, high-profile solicitors like Gareth Peirce[5] and her team of solicitors, plus many barristers, continued to take these cases through the courts year after year, fighting the ghosts of secret evidence on behalf of clients they saw close up enough to know as very different from the popular image.

What happened to these individuals fitted a wider pattern. Dozens of Muslims, with different political and religious backgrounds and from different cultures – Arab, African and South Asian – said to me many times in different words, 'You will never be able to understand the feeling of vulnerability that underlies every aspect of our lives, and the choices we make.' The erosion of refugee rights, violent incidents against foreigners, Islamophobia, especially against veiled Muslim women, and the rise of intolerance in mainstream Britain not only on the far Right, was documented throughout this period in the work of the Institute of Race Relations in London.[6] The weekly news service of IRR chronicled this world of prejudice, injustice and resistance, remote from the images of Britain dominant in the powerful establishment media or the tabloid world of celebrity and scandal.

Across the Atlantic, both Noor and Laila's fathers' cases clearly illustrated their lawyers' bleak conclusion that in the US in recent decades Muslims did not have the First Amendment rights that others US citizens did. If they publicly discussed US foreign policy, or criticised it, as both prominent men did, they opened themselves to investigation and potential prosecution. These were the seminal cases for Patriot Act powers – key pointers for what the South London families feared their sons were facing. While if Muslims undertook the charity work that other religious and secular charities did, they could expect the same – as the Holy Land Foundation case showed when its leadership was indicted, while USAID, among others, was providing aid to the very same institutions.[7]

These double standards had brought fear not only into many Muslim communities, but also, some told me, into the US legal profession, where some lawyers feared taking terrorism-related cases in case they too were targeted. 'The civil liberties community rose up around Guantanamo, focused on the principles of *habeas* and getting people into the federal system. There was much less scrutiny on the *kind* of process – the rights abridgement – that Muslim defendants were actually receiving within the federal system', said Jeanne Theoharis, a professor at Brooklyn College in New York. 'On top of this, the chilling effect of the prosecution of defence lawyer Lynne Stewart and translator (adjunct professor) Mohamed Yousry led to a certain reticence, a fear of being associated with these cases.' (Ms Stewart was the lawyer for the blind Egyptian Sheikh Omar Abdel-Rahman. She was charged with conspiracy to provide material support for terrorism in 2005. She received a ten-year sentence.)

However, top US lawyers did take on the landmark terrorism-related cases of Lynne Stewart, Noor's and Laila's fathers, and the Pakistani neuro-scientist Dr Aafia Siddiqui who received an 86-year sentence for allegedly trying to murder US soldiers. These US lawyers were deeply committed to their clients and certainly did not appear to be afraid of the US government. But they had to come to terms with a fact that often doomed their clients. 'After 9/11 the Constitution was suspended when it comes to Muslims, especially Palestinians', said Linda Moreno, counsel for those three Muslim defendants. And Nancy Hollander, lawyer for another of the HLF defendants – the CEO Shukri Abu Baker who, like Noor's father, got 65 years – said after the sentence, 'I was horrified by it, the thought that somebody gets 65 years for providing charity is really shameful and I believe this case will go down in history, as have others ... as a shameful day. Essentially these people were convicted because they were Palestinians.'[8]

Michael Ratner, president of the Centre for Constitutional Rights, reflecting on a decade of the war on terror, said:

HLF, Al Arian – its all of a piece. After 9/11 it hasn't been about terrorists, but about Muslims. Wire-taps, round-ups, torture, entrapment ... and HLF was going after Muslim civil society. It's now very very difficult for Muslims to organize anything, or speak up. I think about Germany, how did it happen? Well, we're not there yet, but we can see how a population can be silenced ... and a population scape-goated.

The late Howard Zinn summed up the climate of the early twenty-first century in the US.

The so-called 'war on terror' has been, from the first, a war against the rights of people in this country, and indeed is itself an act of terrorism against people who now have to be afraid of engaging in any act, or uttering any words, that offend the government. This is not the behaviour of a democracy but of a totalitarian state.[9]

The majority of people in the US who agreed to talk to me openly about the cases in this book trusted me to keep their anonymity. In this atmosphere, the bravery of Noor, Laila,

Sonali and Mariam, in constantly speaking out publicly for their fathers and their brothers, is extraordinarily impressive and testimony to the values of their families.

Some fervent words of one of the young women in Britain summed up what many, though far from all, of the other women in this book said to me, often:

> Thank Allah for everything that's happened, the best judge is Allah, he will give the innocents their rights, not the unfair judges and government. Everything from Allah has his mercy in it, and we are not sad since we had the bad news, believe me, we keep thanking Allah.

Her words encapsulated the distance between these women and the societies that had treated them with such cruelty and injustice – because of who their relations were.

Several of these men face very serious charges – more than 200 murders in the case of Adel Abdul Bary, or bank-rolling of Islamic *jihad* in Palestine in the case of Sami Al Arian, or links to Al Qaeda terrorist plots where many people died, and influencing others to participate in *jihad*, in the case of Abu Qatada and others. Politicians, judges, police and intelligence services have repeatedly described them as dangerous to people living in the US or Britain – some dangerous enough to be denied bail to house arrest. Those reports of potential danger have been an unquestioned theme in the media for a decade.

Between the gravity of the charges the men face and the wives' perception of the lives their husbands lived before the charges were made there is a vast discrepancy and unbridgeable incomprehension. Almost all of these women, even those living largely segregated lives, who might be thought unworldly by Western standards, are women who believe they know their husbands inside out, with no illusions, no mysteries. No one can, they believe, know things about these men that they do not know.

For these women the years passed with very few details ever emerging concerning the evidence held against the men, which made them believed to be so dangerous. Secret evidence, or anonymous witnesses, was a common thread in most of the cases, in the US as well as in the UK. 'Material support for terrorism' or 'links to known terrorists' were frustratingly vague charges to all the families. All the women saw these accusations as shields either for the Islamophobia they lived with daily and which they believed would prefer them out of the country, or as part of a deal involving the UK and US authorities and the Arab regimes from which the men fled.

The real societies and linked powers of Britain and the United States, and the once imagined worlds of a pure Islamic Afghanistan and of a nation state in Palestine, are the clashing visions which underlay almost all the stories of the women in this book. Most of those who went to Afghanistan believed they were living differently, making sacrifices, to help in creating a better world. 'It wasn't just hopes – we did create an international community which we were proud of and believed in – that was what all the well-digging and school-building was about.' The Palestinians, like almost all Palestinians in the diaspora, believed always in keeping faith with the struggle for a just Palestinian state – and speaking out for the Palestinian right to justice – whatever the cost in their adopted societies.

Neither of these imagined worlds – an Afghanistan and a Palestine – ever represented a threat to the West. A perceived or an invented threat lies behind every story in this book. The threat and reality of terrorism came from somewhere else – deluded, marginalised men who believed violence was a short-cut to political change in their own societies and the Western societies allied with their rulers. Joseph Conrad's nineteenth-century novel, *The Secret Agent*, with its anarchist group well known to the police, agent provocateur, use of violence to produce outrage and excuse repression, death of an innocent, was a microcosm which contained all the elements of the post 9/11 world.

Yet the scale of the early twenty-first-century events was so big, and the pattern so complex, that the actual details of what happened in people's lives, and with that some understanding of the costs, were mostly invisible. The Bush administration's decision to launch the war on terror, instead of using the police, intelligence and, above all, the legal system, set the course for the world of destroyed societies in the East, a burning sense of injustice across much of the globe and the void of intellectual and moral values in the mainstream West.

As Paul Fussell wrote of the First World War, 'Every war is ironic, because every war is worse than expected. Every war constitutes an irony of situation, because its means are melo-dramatically disproportionate to its ends.'[10]

From the US war on terror – on-going, although the phrase was dropped by President Obama – what have been the costs in the UK and the US, to society and to the legal system which is supposed to represent the best values of society, of the practices that have deformed so many family lives in the last dozen years in the two countries? The American lawyers cited here have given their harsh judgements. But the full price is one that no one can yet weigh, though history will surely judge it, as Fussell said, as melodramatically disproportionate.

Almost all the women in this book lived lives in which a harsh everyday reality, and the injustice suffered in the UK or the US in these years, was intertwined with memories, ghosts and dreams of an Afghanistan or a Palestine – past or future. These other shadow lives infused everything for them, if you came close enough to listen, and were, with their faith, their secret lifeline of joy and resilience against bitterness and despair.

Afterword

Marina Warner

The profession has been shamed recently, exposed for its venality and unscrupulousness, but the work of a reporter and commentator like Victoria Brittain returns journalism to its role in a country where we vaunt our right to freedom of speech, and condescend to other nations who do not enjoy such liberty, to whom we wish to set an example of democracy in action. She takes up the historic, adversarial, difficult part of the critic who keeps vigil over power, of the sharp-eyed observer who notices what has not been said, who looks in places where nobody has ventured. She is brave, she has been toughened by experience and she speaks up on behalf of individuals who represent elements that are so unpopular they have been buried beyond notice. Her writing makes us look at subjects that embarrass us: at Muslim piety, veiled women, at the mothers, wives, sisters and children of suspected *jihadists*. These are among the members of British society whom most of us pass by, askance, uncomprehending, wishing they would not wear that face mask or have so many children or want to pray so often. *Shadow Lives* makes us look again, by taking a line of sight at an angle, and acknowledge the dignity and perseverance and survival skills of individuals under extreme pressure – in many cases with the absence of the paterfamilias and chief breadwinner, very straitened means and the perennial threat of social ostracism.

Victoria Brittain has kept company with the families in the book and listened to their life stories, read their pleas and their poems and stood by them in hard times. She introduces us to Ragaa, the wife of Adel Abdul Bary the lawyer; Farida, the mother of Talha Ahsan the poet; Sabiha, the mother, and Amna, the sister, of Babar Ahmed, the computer engineer, and to several others. In some cases, she has preserved her subjects' anonymity. Several women in the book are related to men who have been arrested and re-arrested in the round-ups after 9/11, and are, or were, in prisons here and in the US, including Guantanamo.

She has seen their children grow up; the children's own babies born; grandparents become ill and frail; some marriages fail and some women break down under the strain. She has waited up with them for news and celebrated with them when there has been cause. Her testimony is an act of ordinary human sympathy – recognition of the bonds that make us alike rather than the forces that alienate us. Like Wilfred Owen in the dark tunnels of his dream, she meets the other and knows her – 'I knew you in this dark, my friend'.

The Meaning of Waiting is the title of the music theatre piece that Victoria Brittain wrote two years ago, about the wives and families of men who were held on suspicion of terrorism, and specifically of involvement with Al Qaeda. They were waiting for verdicts, for the men's return, for reprieve – or for the worst. She waited with them, and continued to do so, because cases remained unsettled for many years: Adel Abdul Bary was first taken 14 years ago; Syed Talha Ahsan in 2006 and Babar Ahmed in 2003. The suspects were held without charge in high security prisons, in Belmarsh or in Long Lartin. When the flouting of Habeas Corpus became too flagrant, some were released home under Control Orders. Victoria Brittain continued to wait, and now, since she finished this book, the waiting (for them) is over for three of the families she writes about here, at least for this long phase. On 5 October 2012 the detainees were extradited to the US to be tried there.

Shadow Lives unfolds dilemmas for civil society and makes us face the tensions in liberal precepts. But we need uncomfortable books like this one, to ask the tough questions.

Her friends – for some of the women have become friends – find that their religious faith gives them comfort; they draw the power to be patient and forbearing from it. It gives them strength to endure and hope – just as it does Christians and no doubt members of other faiths. Those of us with secular convictions, who recoil from the hegemony of any church, may not like this, but belief is no longer simply a matter of private conscience. It has become an intrinsic dynamic in politics: it is the case that some faith schools in the UK now accept pupils only on proof of parents' church attendance; in Russia, heavy punishment is being meted out to Pussy Riot for blasphemy; and in the US, a devout Mormon was the Republican contender for the Presidency in a tight election. We cannot afford to be contemptuous of people's piety and of the power of the mosques over their congregations and to think complacently of them as deeply other. We need to work out a new approach to religious allegiance in order to maintain civil life and freedoms – and it will take philosophers less reductive than the militant atheists and less wavering than the last Archbishop of Canterbury to do it. If a vacuum grows at the heart of our institutions – an ineffective parliament, an undermined judiciary – then these religious forces of all kinds will struggle for supremacy to fill it, as we are seeing, for example, in the countries of the Arab Spring, where the contending factions within Islam have arisen as a consequence of the corruption of government and state institutions, such as the law, over the decades of misrule.

The answer must be to strengthen the structural institutions of democracy, including the relations between public protest and the press. This is the second point that emerges from this open-eyed book: the reporting in the media on the suspects and on their imprisonment did not represent the ordeals they were put through or the strength of the outcry against it and against deportation. And after four of the detainees were lumped together with Abu Hamza as if they were a single case, even the normally responsible *Today* programme on BBC radio overlooked the differences between them (Abu Hamza was convicted and sentenced for crimes he had committed; the others have never been charged in the UK since no evidence could be found). Yet John Humphrys, interviewing Theresa May (6 October 2012), seemed to think that the extradition process had taken such a long time through sheer disorganisation or bloody-mindedness, not because the lawyers had grounds for opposing the US demand and the judges in several courts had upheld their objections.

Victoria Brittain's book reveals the deep historical background very tellingly and it is a bitter story. The families come from different parts of the globe and from different kinds of social background, and they became British because they were given legal refugee status here either from dictatorships or after the tumult in the world – above all the changed policies in Afghanistan and Pakistan – placed them or their fathers or husbands in danger. At the end of the 1980s they came to the UK as to a haven, a lawful and welcoming shelter where justice and freedom were observed. As Mary Robinson has stated, it is essential that we battle to uphold that tradition of human rights, because if standards continue to fall in the old democracies of the West, then permission is given to abandon principles elsewhere. This is the third issue that the quiet, stoical, determined women in this book illuminate: that those suspected of terrorism could not be tried here in a British court raises the most acute concern about legal processes in a globalised polity.

Putting to the fore the broader issues that Victoria Brittain diagnoses does not, however, do justice to the dramatic human picture she preser — of extraordinary loyalty and discretion, of children who must ke quiet about their weekend visits to their father in gaol, of the strain th sometimes, has ended a marriage or driven a young wife mad.

A fourth and final point arises directly from the intimacy of approach to her notorious subjects' families. What about the generation? What does this moment of crisis in British legal indepen and multi-ethnic society mean for young Muslims growing up? For above all, it is vital to keep faith with the highest principles of our national tradition and not dishonour them. This would be the case if the detainees had been charged with a crime or crimes; even more so when they have not been. I was reminded of Joan of Arc: one of the principal reasons she became a heroine known throughout the world is because she stands for those who resist persecution. She was not allowed to hear the evidence against her and died at the stake after a trial in which she did not know what she was charged with, and she has become a popular saint fought over by different factions to justify their cause. Illegality has a way of coming back to haunt you, sometimes for centuries.

The situation of the detainees is generically Kafkaesque, as many have pointed out. But there is one fable of Kafka's which is not as well known as others, which especially relates to the response to 9/11 and the wars in Iraq and Afghanistan: 'Jackals and Arabs', in which the two are locked in a continual collusion of violence.

One jackal comes trotting up to the 'European' narrator with 'a small pair of sewing scissors, covered with ancient rust, dangling from an eyetooth', and invites him to use it to slit an Arab's throat. The spokesman of the Arabs explains the protracted, endless enmity that drives the pack of jackals: '"it's common knowledge; so long as Arabs exist, that pair of scissors goes wandering through the desert and will wander with us to the end of our days. Every European is offered it for the great work … They have the most lunatic hopes, these beasts…"'

At the close of the story, the Arab tosses the jackals the carcass of a dead camel and, with the European beside him, watches as the pack tear it to pieces. The Arab lashes them with his whip but they come back for more blood, until the narrator, '… stayed his arm. "You are right, sir," said he, "we'll leave them to their business…"'

In this story, written in 1917, Kafka is transmuting the frenzy and blood lust of the First World War into an Aesopian parable. But as with so much else that this writer wrote, he seems to be prophesying, for his vision here scathes so fiercely the vicious circle of animosity fuelled by repeated, short-term violent solutions. The last line is, '"Marvellous creatures, aren't they? And how they hate us!"'*

Shadow Lives by Victoria Brittain is a courageous example of 'soft power', if that phrase means mutual exchanges and understanding rather than bellicose intolerance; she is unusual, generous and imaginative in attempting to break the hypnotic hold of mutual antagonism and to give us a glimpse into the lives of others.

---

*   Franz Kafka, 'Jackals and Arabs', in *The Complete Short Stories of Franz Kafka*, trans. Willa and Edwin Muir (London [1933]: Vintage, 1999), pp. 407–11.

Notes

INTRODUCTION

1. All quotations from family members and from lawyers are from personal conversations with the author between 2003 and 2012, unless otherwise stated.
2. Nick Turse, 'Tomgram: Nick Turse, Prisons, Drones, and Black Ops in Afghanistan', 12 February 2012, www.tomdispatch.com/post/175501/tomgram%3A_nick_turse%2C_prisons%2C_drones%2C_and_black_ops_in_afghanistan/ (last accessed 2 July 2012).
3. Roger Hardy, *The Muslim Revolt*, London: Hurst, 2010, p. 39.
4. Mohamed Heikal, *Autumn of Fury*, London: Andre Deutsch, 1983, p. 227.
5. Interview with Brzezinski in *Nouvelle Observateur*, Paris, 15–21 January 1998.
6. Ibid.
7. Victoria Brittain, *The Meaning of Waiting* (play), London: Oberon Books, 2010, p. 22.
8. John Stockwell, *In Search of Enemies: How the CIA Lost Angola*, London: Andre Deutsch, 1978, and Victoria Brittain, *Death of Dignity*, London: Pluto, 1998.
9. Brittain, *The Meaning of Waiting*, p. 24.
10. Moazzam Begg, *Enemy Combatant*, London: Simon and Schuster, 2005, p. 46.
11. Lakhdar Boumediene, 'My Guantanamo Nightmare', *New York Times*, 7 January 2012; Marc Perelman, 'From Sarajevo to Guantanamo: The Strange Case of the Algerian Six', *Mother Jones*, 4 December 2007.
12. Ken Keable (ed.), *London Recruits: The Secret War Against Apartheid*, London: Merlin, 2012.
13. Baya Gacemi, *Moi, Nadia, femme d'un emir du GIA*, Paris: Editions du Seuil, 1998, trans. Paul Cote and Constantina Mitchell, *I, Nadia, Wife of a Terrorist*, Lincoln, NE: University of Nebraska Press, 2006.
14. Anthony Shadid, 'Arab Spring's Hope Rose from Deep Roots', *New York Times*, 18 February 2012.
15. Azzam Tamimi (ed.), *Power-Sharing Islam*, London: Liberty, 1993, p. 62.

16. Shadid, 'Arab Spring's Hope Rose from Deep Roots'.
17. National Commission on Terrorist Attacks, *The 9/11 Commission Report*, New York: Norton, 2004, p. 153.
18. National Commission on Terrorist Attacks, *The 9/11 Commission Report*, p. 152.
19. Syed Saleem Shahzad, *Inside Al-Qaeda and the Taliban*, London: Pluto, 2011.
20. Steve Coll, *The New Yorker*, 12 December 2005, p. 48.
21. Lawrence Wright, *The Looming Tower*, New York: Knopf, 2006, p. 260.
22. Jane Mayer, *The Dark Side*, New York: Doubleday, 2008, p. 116.
23. Wright, *The Looming Tower*, p. 197.
24. Abdul Salam Zaeef, *My Life with the Taliban*, London: Hurst, 2010, pp. 142–6.
25. Joseph Margulies, *Guantanamo and the Abuse of Presidential Power*, New York: Simon and Schuster, 2007, p. 3.
26. Elaine Hagopian (ed.), *Civil Rights in Peril*, London: Pluto, 2004, p. 22.
27. Hagopian, *Civil Rights in Peril*, p. 31.
28. Gareth Peirce, *Dispatches from the Dark Side*, London: Verso, 2010, p. 3.
29. Michael Ratner, *The Trial of Donald Rumsfeld*, New York: The New Press, 2008, p. 13.
30. Margulies, *Guantanamo*, p. 22.
31. Peirce, *Dispatches from the Dark Side*, p. 30.
32. Andy Worthington, 'How to Read WikiLeaks' Guantánamo Files', 1 May 2011, www.andyworthington.co.uk/2011/05/01/how-to-read-wikileaks-guantanamo-files/ (last accessed 2 July 2012).
33. Seton Hall Center for Policy and Research, *Guantánamo Reports*, http://law.shu.edu/programscenters/publicintgovserv/policyresearch/guantanamo-reports.cfm (last accessed 2 July 2012).
34. Zaeef, *My Life with the Taliban*, pp. 136–9.
35. Mark P. Denbeaux, *The 14 Myths of Guantánamo*, Seton Hall Law School, 2007, http://law.shu.edu/publications/guantanamoReports/fourteen_myths_of_gtmo_final.pdf (last accessed 2 July 2012).
36. Interview, 2012.
37. Margulies, *Guantanamo*, p. 11.
38. Margulies, *Guantanamo*, p. 14.
39. Hagopian, *Civil Rights in Peril*, pp. 236–8.
40. Sara Roy, *Hamas and Civil Society in Gaza*, Princeton, NJ: Princeton University Press, 2011, p. 100.

41. *Los Angeles Times*, 26 February 2009; *Independent*, 7 December 2010; *Guardian*, 20 March 2012.
42. Peirce, *Dispatches from the Dark Side*, p. 124 (updated 2012 edition).
43. Frank Lind was filmed in the web project, http://witnesstoguantanamo. com/ (last accessed 9 October 2012).

CHAPTER 1

1. Author notes taken in court.

CHAPTER 2

1. Victoria Brittain, *The Meaning of Waiting* (play), London: Oberon Books, 2010, p. 50.
2. Brittain, *The Meaning of Waiting*, p. 49.

CHAPTER 3

1. Peirce, *Dispatches from the Dark Side*, London: Verso, 2010, p. 30.
2. *Guardian*, 26 February 2004.
3. Peirce, *Dispatches from the Dark Side*, p. 31.
4. I. Robbins, J. MacKeith, S. Davison, M. Kopelman, C. Meux, S. Ratnam, D. Somekh and R. Taylor, 'The Psychiatric Problems of Detainees under the 2001 Anti-Terrorism Crime and Security Act', *The Psychiatrist*, Vol. 29, No. 11, 2005, p. 408.
5. Brian Barder, 'Brian Barder Explains Why He Resigned from the Special Immigration Appeals Commission', *London Review of Books*, Vol. 26, No. 6, 2004, www.lrb.co.uk/v26/n06/brian-barder/ on-siac (last accessed 2 July 2012).
6. Ibid.
7. Letters written by various children living under Control Orders in 2009.

CHAPTER 4

1. Victoria Brittain, *The Meaning of Waiting* (play), London: Oberon Books, 2010, pp. 22–3.

CHAPTER 5

1. Mohamed Heikal, *Autumn of Fury*, London: Andre Deutsch, 1983, p. 241.

CHAPTER 7

1. American Civil Liberties Union (ACLU), *Blocking Faith, Freezing Charity*, June 2009, p. 53.
2. ACLU, *Blocking Faith*, p. 63.
3. Nancy Hollander, *Democracy Now*, 29 May 2009.
4. ACLU, *Blocking Faith*, p. 53.
5. Amnesty International, December 2005.
6. Glenn Greenwald, 'Personalising Civil Liberties Abuses', *Salon*, 16 April 2012. ww.salon.com/2012/04/16/personalizing_civil_liberties_abuses/ (last accessed 2 July 2012).

CHAPTER 8

1. Y. Bedjaoui, A. Aroua and M. Ait-Larbi (eds), *An Inquiry into the Algerian Massacres*, Geneva: Hoggar Books, 1999, p. 9. Also Hichem Aboud, *La Mafia des Genéréax*, Paris: J.C. Lattes, 2002.
2. Ms Moreno represented Noor's father in the HLF case, and actually moved to Dallas for a year to prepare the case because of its extreme complexity and importance.
3. Line Halvorsen, *USA vs Al Arian*, 2007 (film, Norway).
4. Sally Neighbour, *The Mother of Mohammed*, Melbourne: Melbourne University Press, 2009, pp. 174–85 on women's life in Peshawar in the 1990s and see p. 256 for life in 2001 in Kabul under the Taliban from the perspective of Rabiah Hutchinson, a Western woman living there.
5. Gareth Peirce, *Dispatches from the Dark Side*, London: Verso, 2010.
6. Liz Fekete, *A Suitable Enemy: Racism, Migration and Islamophobia in Europe*, London: Pluto, 2009 and Milly Williamson and Gholam Khiabany, 'UK: The Veil and the Politics of Racism', *Race and Class*, Vol. 52, No. 2, 2010, pp. 85–96.
7. Lawyer Chase Madar, Fordham School of Law, 16 March 2012, http://law.fordham.edu/25655.htm (last accessed 9 October 2012) and HLF defence lawyer John Cline, quoted in Counterpunch, 31 August 2011, www.counterpunch.org (last accessed 9 October 2012).
8. *Democracy Now*, 29 May 2009.
9. www.howardzinn.org, 4 August 2008 (last accessed 9 October 2012).
10. Paul Fussell, *The Great War and Modern Memory*, New York: Oxford University Press, 1974.

Select Bibliography

Al Ghazali, Zainab, *Return of the Pharaoh*, Leicester: The Islamic Foundation, 2006.

de Bellaigue, Christopher, *In the Rose Garden of the Martyrs: A Memoir of Iran*, London: Harper Collins, 2004.

Brittain, Victoria, *The Meaning of Waiting* (play), London: Oberon Books, 2010.

Clark, Ramsey, Zangana, Haifa and Reifer, Thomas, *The Torturer in the Mirror*, New York: Seven Stories Press, 2010.

Danner, Mark, *Torture and Truth*, London: Granta Books, 2004.

Gacemi, Baya, *Moi, Nadia, femme d'un emir du GIA*, Paris: Editions du Seuil, 1998, trans. Paul Cote and Constantina Mitchell, *I, Nadia, Wife of a Terrorist*, Lincoln, NE: University of Nebraska Press, 2006.

Greenberg, Karen and Dratel, Joshua (eds), *The Torture Papers*, Cambridge: Cambridge University Press, 2005.

Hagopian, Elaine (ed.), *Civil Rights in Peril*, London: Pluto, 2004.

Hardy, Roger, *The Muslim Revolt*, London: Hurst, 2010.

Heikal, Mohamed, *Autumn of Fury*, London: Andre Deutsch, 1983.

Margulies, Joseph, *Guantanamo and the Abuse of Presidential Power*, New York: Simon and Schuster, 2007.

Mayer, Jane, *The Dark Side*, New York: Doubleday, 2008.

Nasiri, Omar, *Inside the Jihad*, New York: Basic Books, 2006.

National Commission on Terrorist Attacks, *The 9/11 Commission Report*, New York: Norton, 2004.

Neighbour, Sally, *The Mother of Mohammed*, Melbourne: Melbourne University Press, 2009.

Peirce, Gareth, *Dispatches from the Dark Side*, London: Verso, 2010.

Qureshi, Asim, *Rules of the Game*, London: Hurst, 2009.

Ratner, Michael, *The Trial of Donald Rumsfeld*, New York: The New Press, 2008.

Rogan, Eugene, *The Arabs*, London: Allen Lane, 2009.

Roy, Sara, *Hamas and Civil Society in Gaza*, Princeton, NJ: Princeton University Press, 2011.

Shadid, Anthony, *Legacy of the Prophet, Despots, Democrats and the New Politics of Islam*, Boulder, CO: Westview, 2002.

Shahzad, Syed Saleem, *Inside Al-Qaeda and the Taliban*, London: Pluto, 2011.

Wright, Lawrence, *The Looming Tower*, New York: Knopf, 2006.

Zaeef, Abdul Salam, *My Life with the Taliban*, London: Hurst, 2010.

Index

Compiled by Sue Carlton

7/7 London bombings 6, 20, 58, 71
9/11 terrorist attacks 1, 9, 20, 71
  and intelligence swoop on Muslims 6, 26, 29, 51, 114
  US response to 12–14, 16, 123
  see also intelligence fishing net; war on terror

Aamer, Shaker 42–9
  campaign to release 46–7
  capture 44–5
  cleared for release 47
  decision to move to Afghanistan 42–3
  wife of *see* Zinnira
Abd al-Hamid Kishk, Sheikh 84
Abdel-Rahman, Sheikh Omar 9, 156, 160
Abdul Bary, Adel 10–11, 84–8, 156, 162
  arrests in London 87–8
  extradition case 11, 81, 88, 91–2, 96, 156
  on hunger strike 93–4
  imprisonment and torture in Egypt 84–5
  response to revolution in Egypt 94, 96
  wife and family *see* Ragaa
Abu Ali, Ahmed 132–8
  appeal (2012) 135
  charges in US 132, 133–4
  family 134–5, 137–8
  imprisonment in Saudi Arabia 132–3, 134
  torture 132, 133

Abu Ali, Mariam (sister of Ahmed Abu Ali) 132–8, 162
  education 135, 145
  finding a job 135
  marriage 136
  publicity for Ahmed's case 135–6
Abu Baker, Shukri 18, 161
Abu Ghraib prison 16, 29
Abu Marzook, Mousa 122, 123
Abu Qatada 71, 114–21, 162
  children of 113–17, 118, 121
  friendship with el Banna 28, 31
  imprisonment and torture in Jordan 114, 117
  rearrest (2008) 119
  refused bail 158–9
  release on bail (2008) 118
  release on bail (2012) 120–1
  wife of 117–18
Afghanistan 1–2, 5, 43
  Muslim immigration 7–8, 163
  targeted after US embassy bombings 10
  womens' memories of 153–4
African National Congress (ANC) 7
Ahmed, Amna (sister of Babar Ahmed) 104–5, 107, 108, 110, 112
Ahmed, Ashfaq (Babar's father) 107, 108, 111, 112
Ahmed, Babar 6, 104–12
  arrest 105–6
  case against Metropolitan police 106–7, 112
  family background 107–9

Ahmed, Babar *continued*
   fighting extradition 104, 106,
      109–10
   mother of *see* Sabiha
   wife and marriage 105–6, 110,
      111–12
Ahsan, Farida (mother of Talha
   Ahsan) 98–101, 102–3
Ahsan, Hamja 99, 101–2
Ahsan, Talha 98–104
   academic interests and career
      101, 102–3
   community work 103
   family background 99–101,
      102
   imprisonment fighting
      extradition 98–9, 101–2,
      103–4
Algeria 2, 6, 7, 8–9, 140
American Civil Liberties Union
   (ACLU) 124–5
Amnesty International 35, 86,
   112
anti-terrorist laws 1, 13, 14–15
   see also bail conditions;
      Control Orders
Antiterrorism and Effective Death
   Penalty Act 13
Arab Spring 2–3, 91, 153
   see also Egypt, revolution
      (2011)
Arab–Israeli war (1967) 3
Al Arian, Laila (daughter of Sami
   Al Arian) 134, 145–7,
      148–52, 161–2
   and journalism 149–50
Al Arian, Sami 18, 133–4, 145–8,
      149–50, 162
   acquittal by jury 18, 150
   imprisonment 148
   as lobbyist on Arab/American
      issues 146–7
   released on bail 150–2
Ashcroft, John 18

Al Aziz, Farouk 19
Azzam.com 99, 104

Bagram 14, 17, 32, 44, 68, 113
bail conditions 53, 59–60, 118,
   139–40
   see also Control Orders;
      electronic tagging
Bangla language 98, 101, 102
Bangladesh 98, 103
el Banna, Anas 24–5, 32, 35
el Banna, Jamil 24–40
   imprisonment 29–32
   interrogations 31
   Spanish extradition warrant
      38–40
   trip to Gambia 28–9
   wife of *see* Sabah
Barder, Sir Brian 54
Begg, Moazzam 30, 43, 45–6,
      50–1, 112
   prison memoirs 68
   wife of *see* Zeynab
Belmarsh prison 15, 52–3
   letters from prisoners to
      Guardian 52
   prisoners with mental illness
      52–3, 56, 73
Bin Laden, Osama 8, 9, 10, 11,
      12, 91, 92
Blair, Tony 2, 12–13, 20, 24–5
Blunkett, David 120
Bojinka plot 9, 20
Borgen, Erling 15
Bosnia 6, 7, 8
Boumediene, Houari 7
Bourgiba, Habib 8
Britain
   anti-terrorism legislation
      14–15, 105
   see also bail conditions;
      Control Orders; electronic
      tagging
   data collection on Muslims 29

Golden Jubilee celebrations
155
and Islamist politics 8
Islamophobia 16, 20–1, 114,
159, 163
Olympic Games (2012) 155
request for Jamil and Omar to
be returned 38
terrorist attacks *see* 7/7
London bombings
Broadmoor Secure Mental
Hospital 33, 51, 53, 56–7,
77
Brzezinski, Zbigniew 4
Bush, George W. 2, 123, 132,
146, 147
response to 9/11 attack 12–13
see also United States (US),
Bush administration
Bush, Jeb 147

Camp David negotiations (1978)
3
Carter, Jimmy 4
Centre for Constitutional Rights
(CCR) 16, 161
Charles, Prince 24–5
Chechens 142–3
Chechnya 6, 7, 8, 142, 143
children, in Control Order
families 21–2, 63–5, 87
Clinton, Bill 13, 146
Clinton, Hillary 146
Cold War 4, 23
Collins, Judge 57
Combatant Status Review
Tribunal 31–2
Communications Management
Units (CMUs) 19, 23, 127,
129
confession, under torture 132,
133
Conrad, Joseph 163

Control Orders 21, 50, 51, 53–4,
58–9, 63–4, 68, 153
Council on American-Islamic
Relations (CAIR) 123
curfews 8, 39–40, 60, 63, 118,
120, 139–40

Davey, Ed 32
Death in Guantanamo 15
Deghayes, Omar 36, 37, 38
Denbeaux, Mark 15–16
deportation 54, 63, 143, 150
bail pending 8, 78, 119, 139
contesting 38, 54, 78, 81, 93
and fear of torture 14–15, 32,
51, 63, 139
Dhafir, Dr Rafil 18
Dina (wife of Mahmoud) 5–6,
55, 56–7, 62–7

education 119, 130, 145–6
haram (forbidden) 84
Eggers, Dave 128
Egypt 2–3, 78–9, 90, 146
and Islamist politics 10–11, 12
life under Sadat regime 81–6
relations with Israel 3
revolution 2011 2, 81, 91, 94,
96–7, 156
Egyptian Islamic Jihad (EIJ) 9,
10, 11
Eid holidays 34, 35–6, 111, 139
Elashi, Ghassan 123–8
imprisonment 18, 124, 127–8
trials 123–4, 125, 126–7
see also Holy Land Foundation
Elashi, Nadia (cousin of Ghassan
Elashi) 123
Elashi, Noor (daughter of
Ghassan Elashi) 19–20,
121–8, 129, 161–2
campaign for father's release
126–8
decision to remove *hijab* 128

Elashi, Noor *continued*
    education 123, 127, 145
    family background 122–3
    refused entry to Palestine
        125–6
electronic tagging 39, 57, 60, 63,
    118, 139, 144
Elphicke, Charlie 120
En Nahdha party 9
European Court of Human
    Rights (ECHR) 96, 99, 106,
    120, 156, 157
evidence
    anonymous witnesses 11, 163
    obtained by torture 15, 32,
        114, 120, 132, 133
    secret 8, 51, 52, 119, 140, 146,
        147, 158, 159, 163
extradition
    appeals against 157–8
    requests from US 98–9, 121–2,
        139, 156–7
    see also under individual
        suspects

Facebook 102, 135
al Fadl, Jamal Ahmed 11–12, 92
FBI, infiltrating mosques 12, 16,
    19, 133
Ferjani, Said 8
Finsbury Park mosque 71, 141
Fitzgerald, Edward 39
Free Babar Ahmed campaign
    105, 107
Freedomtogive.com 127–8
Fussell, Paul 164

Gambia, el Banna's trip to 24, 25,
    28–9, 31, 32, 36
Garzon, Judge Balthazar 39
Gaza Strip, community
    organisations funding 123–4
Geneva Conventions 13
Ghailani, Ahmed 92

Ghannouchi, Sheikh Rashid 8–9
Ghurab, Nizar 156
Gore, Al 146
Greenwald, Glen 133–4
Grozny 8
Guantanamo Bay prison 6, 12,
    15–18, 24–40
    legal challenges to detentions
        16–17
    over-riding international law
        13, 14, 160
    Seton Hall research 15–16
    use of torture 13, 14, 44
    Wikileaks files 15
    *Guantanamo, Honour Bound to
        Defend Freedom* (Tricycle
        Theatre production) 24, 25
Guardian, prisoners' letters to 52
Gulf War (1990–91) 5, 70

Hajj pilgrimage 27, 42
Hamas 18, 122, 123, 124
Hamda (wife of Mr OO) 4,
    69–71, 73–80
    son-in-law imprisoned in Egypt
        78–9
    visit to Jordan 79–80
Heikal, Mohamed 81
Helmand 2
Help the Needy 18
Herat 2
hijab 27, 40, 61, 77, 83, 128,
    151
Hollander, Nancy 161
Holy Land Foundation (HLF) 18,
    121–2, 123, 124–5, 126–7,
    133, 160
hunger strikes 45, 46, 51, 55, 56,
    65–6, 93–4

incapacity benefits 95
India, Partition (1947) 98, 108
INFOMCOM 123
Institute of Race Relations 159

intelligence fishing net 6, 13, 14, 23, 26, 88
International Brigades 7
'International Islamic Front for Jihad against Jews and Crusaders' (1998) 9, 10, 11
International Office for the Defence of the Egyptian People 91
Iqbal, Asif 32
Iran 3
Iranian revolution (1979) 3
Iraq 5, 20, 22, 72
  see also Abu Ghraib prison; Gulf War (1990–91)
Islamic Group (IG) 10–11
Islamophobia 16, 20–1, 114, 159, 163
Israel 3, 17, 27, 34, 56, 145

Jennings, Mark 32
jihad 5, 11, 162
Jordan 2, 70–1
  deportation to 32, 37, 63, 68, 74, 78, 114, 120
  use of torture 71, 72, 77, 117
Josephine (wife of Algerian prisoner) 55, 57–62, 153
justice system 19, 146–7, 149, 150, 160–1, 164

Kandahar 2, 14, 44
Khaldun training camp 142
Khalid Sheikh Mohammed 9
el-Khalifi, Amine 19
King, Martin Luther 128

lawyers
  and extradition appeals 157
  and terrorism cases 160–1
  working to bring back British prisoners 36–7, 46
Libya 2, 123
Lindh, Frank 23

Lindh, John Walker 23
Long Lartin prison 53, 58, 93, 94, 118, 156

Macdonald, Ian 54
McKinnon, Gary 156
McVeigh, Timothy 13
Mahmoud 50–1, 54, 55, 62–7
  and Control Order 58
  hunger strike 51, 56, 65–6
  sharing cell with Mr OO 73
  suicide attempts 53, 63, 65
  transfer to Broadmoor 56–7
  wife of see Dina
Marion, Illinois 19, 127, 129
Marks and Spencer 34
material support 13, 163
  case against US lawyer 160
  cases against terror suspects 18, 98–9, 123–4, 133, 148
Maududi, Abul Alaa 77
May, Theresa 120
media 120, 150, 159
  hostility to HLF 124
  propagating fear 16, 17, 20, 52, 114, 162
  stereotyping 1–2, 157
Mendez, Juan 157
Mickum, Brent 30
Mittings, Judge 119, 158
Monteilh, Craig 19
Moreno, Linda 133, 147, 150, 161
'mosaic' theory 14, 23
Mr G 57–60, 62, 72
Mr OO 68–74, 76, 78–9
  moved to Broadmoor 77
  return home 78
  son-in-law imprisoned in Egypt 78
  wife of see Hamda
Mr U 139–45
  at Khaldun training camp 142
  campaigning in London for Chechens 142–3

Mr U *continued*
  imprisonment 143–4
  influence of London Islamists
    141
  journey to Afghanistan 141
  medical work in Afghanistan
    142
  move to Britain 140–1
  return to London from
    Afghanistan 142–3
Mubarak, Hosni 10, 78, 82, 96
Muslim Brotherhood 3, 8, 10,
  11, 141

Al-Najjar, Mazen 146–7
al Nashiri, Abd al Rahim 10
Nasser, Gamal Abdel 2–3
Niazi, Amadullah 19

Obama, Barack 17, 164
  letter to 127–8
O'Dwyer, Richard 156
Oklahoma City bombing (1995)
  13
Olympic Games (2012) 155, 158
Omar, Mullah 12
Operation Desert Storm 5
Otty, Tim 39

Pakistan 2, 5–6, 15, 28, 98, 155
Patriot Act (US) 13, 124, 146,
  160
Peirce, Gareth 26, 29–30, 33, 38,
  159
plea bargaining 18, 19, 23, 32,
  139, 150
plexiglass 127, 129, 131, 148
police, raids/house searches 56,
  63, 65, 87, 89, 106, 119,
  144
ayer 27, 32, 37, 92, 115, 116,
  119, 130, 158
oners
  ɪ and poetry 53

letters 30, 46, 91, 138
and mental illness 52–3, 56,
  61, 62, 65, 73, 77
phone calls 19, 26, 56, 91,
  93–4, 115, 127, 129, 138,
  148
solitary confinement 13, 18,
  19, 57, 129, 148
visiting 55–6, 72, 99, 104,
  110–11, 131, 137, 148, 156
see also terrorism suspects

Al Qaeda 6, 9–14, 17, 114
fatal consequences of global
  jihad 11–12
suspects linked to 15–16, 20,
  51, 72, 132, 133, 162
US embassy bombings 87, 92

racism 89, 93, 95, 155
Radio Television Libre Mille
  Collines 150
Ragaa (wife of Adel Abdul Bary)
  11, 81–97, 156, 158
and Adel's imprisonment in UK
  87–92
applications for British
  nationality 90
becoming strict Muslim 83–4
children's lives 89–90, 94–5
dress-making course 92–3
going to university 83
life in London 86–97
reassessment of income support
  95–6
visit to Cairo (2009) 93
Ratner, Michael 16, 17, 161
al Rawi, Bisher 24, 31, 36, 37–8
Red Cross 30, 33, 35, 42, 48, 71
Redgrave, Vanessa 38
refugees
  refugee status 71, 86, 117, 156
  rights of 159
rendition flights 14, 40

Ricin plot 20
Rove, Karl 146
Royal College of Psychiatrists 53
Ruposhi Bangla (Bengali
    bookshop) 98
Rwanda 150

Sabah (wife of Jamil el Banna) 4,
    24–40
  campaigning for husband's
    release 35
  determination of 40
  and husband's imprisonment
    14, 20–32
  letters from Jamil 30
  life in London 28, 32, 33
  phone call to Jamil 35–6
  and prayer 27, 32, 37, 39
  visit from Bisher 37–8
Sabiha (mother of Babar Ahmed)
    107, 108, 109, 110–11
Sadat, Anwar 3, 10, 81–2
Saddam Hussein 5
Sadequee, Shifa 129–32
Sadequee, Sonali (sister of Shifa
    Sadequee) 129–32, 162
Said, Edward 102
Saudi Arabia 2, 4, 9
  use of torture 132, 133
Shadid, Anthony 8, 9
Siddiqui, Dr Aafia 19, 160
Sir Richard Eyre Theatre 40
Skype 48, 79
South Africa 7
South African Communist Party
    7
Soviet–Afghan war (1979–89) 4,
    28
  Muslim returnees from 5–6, 70
Spain, extradition request 37,
    38–40
Special Administrative Measures
    (SAMs) 132
Special Branch 26

Special Immigration Appeals
    Commission (SIAC) 53–4,
    120, 139, 140, 144
  and secret evidence 54, 68, 75,
    119, 158
Stewart, Lynne 160
Sudan 10
Suhrawardy, Huseyn Shaheed 100
SuperMax prisons 19, 91, 105,
    132, 136
Syria 123

Taha, Rifai 11
Taliban 2, 7–8, 16, 43
  condemnation of 9/11 attack 12
Teather, Sarah 35
Tehran embassy hostage crisis
    (1980) 3
Terre Haute, Indiana 19, 23
Terrorism Prevention and
    Investigation Measures
    (TPims) 54–5
terrorism suspects
  anonymity 53–4, 139
  charges against 162
  stigmatisation 52, 55, 63
  see also prisoners
Theoharis, Jeanne 160
torture
  in Abu Ghraib 16, 29
  deportation fears 14–15, 32,
    51, 63, 139
  in Egypt 2, 10, 84–5
  evidence obtained by 15, 32,
    114, 120, 132, 133
  in Jordan 71, 77, 117
  and mental health problems 53
  in Tunisia 9
  US use of 14–15, 29–30, 32, 44
Tunisia 2, 9
Twitter 102, 135

Uighers, refused entry to US 17
UK Border Agency 144

United States (US)
anti-terrorism legislation 13,
  146, 160
Bush administration 14, 15,
  17, 129, 164
  see also Bush, George W.
conviction of terrorist suspects
  18–20
  see also material support
embassy bombings (1998)
  9–10, 87, 91–2
extradition requests 98–9,
  121–2, 139, 156–7
fear of Arabs/Muslims 16, 17
fear of communism 4–5
funding for mujahedeen 4, 5
Muslims' rights 160–1
occupation of Afghanistan 2
proxy wars 5
relations with Egypt 3
use of torture 14–15, 29–30,
  32, 44
violation of international law
  13–15, 17–18
USA v. Usama Bin Laden et al.
  11–12, 91, 92
USAID 124, 160
USS Cole, Al Qaeda attack on 10

war on terror 1–2, 13, 164
effect on justice system 32,
  133, 160–1, 164
families coping with 113,
  139–64
  see also intelligence fishing net

Wikileaks, Guantanamo files 15
women
and charges against relatives
  162–3
impact of Arab Spring 2
leaving Britain 152–3
surviving war on terror
  152–5
UN asset freezing sanctions
  22
Work Capability Assessment
  (WCA) 95
World Trade Center, 1993
  bombing 9

Yemen 10
Yousef, Ramzi 9
Yousry, Mohamed 160

Zaeef, Abdul Salam 12
al Zahrani, Yasser 15
Zakat committees 18, 124
Zawahiri, Ayman 9, 10, 11
Zeynab (wife of Moazzam Begg)
  43, 154
Zinn, Howard 161
Zinnira (wife of Shaker Aamer)
  4, 41–50
letter from Shaker 46
and mental illness 44, 47–8
move to Afghanistan 42–3
move to Pakistan 43–4
poem 49
Skype call to Shaker 48
al-Zomor, Abboud 81